THE PICTURE OF DORIAN GRAY

Oscar Wilde

EDITORIAL DIRECTOR Laurie Barnett
DIRECTOR OF TECHNOLOGY Tammy Hepps

SERIES EDITOR John Crowther
MANAGING EDITOR Vincent Janoski

WRITERS Ross Douthat, David Hopson
EDITORS Benjamin Morgan, Dennis Quinio

This edition published by Spark Publishing

Spark Publishing
A Division of SparkNotes LLC
120 Fifth Avenue, 8th Floor
New York, NY 10011

Please submit all comments and questions or report errors to www.sparknotes.com/errors

Printed and bound in the United States

ISBN 1-58663-485-2

Introduction:
Stopping to Buy SparkNotes on a Snowy Evening

Whose words these are you *think* you know.
Your paper's due tomorrow, though;
We're glad to see you stopping here
To get some help before you go.

Lost your course? You'll find it here.
Face tests and essays without fear.
Between the words, good grades at stake:
Get great results throughout the year.

Once school bells caused your heart to quake
As teachers circled each mistake.
Use SparkNotes and no longer weep,
Ace every single test you take.

Yes, books are lovely, dark, and deep,
But only what you grasp you keep,
With hours to go before you sleep,
With hours to go before you sleep.

Contents

Context

OSCAR WILDE WAS BORN on October 16, 1854, in Dublin, Ireland. He was educated at Trinity College in Dublin and at Magdalen College, Oxford, and settled in London, where he married Constance Lloyd in 1884. In the literary world of Victorian London, Wilde fell in with an artistic crowd that included W. B. Yeats, the great Irish poet, and Lillie Langtry, mistress to the Prince of Wales. A great conversationalist and a famous wit, Wilde began by publishing mediocre poetry but soon achieved widespread fame for his comic plays. The first, *Vera; or, The Nihilists,* was published in 1880. Wilde followed this work with *Lady Windermere's Fan* (1892), *A Woman of No Importance* (1893), *An Ideal Husband* (1895), and his most famous play, *The Importance of Being Earnest* (1895). Although these plays relied upon relatively simple and familiar plots, they rose well above convention with their brilliant dialogue and biting satire.

Wilde published his only novel, *The Picture of Dorian Gray,* before he reached the height of his fame. The first edition appeared in the summer of 1890 in *Lippincott's Monthly Magazine.* It was criticized as scandalous and immoral. Disappointed with its reception, Wilde revised the novel in 1891, adding a preface and six new chapters. The Preface (as Wilde calls it) anticipates some of the criticism that might be leveled at the novel and answers critics who charge *The Picture of Dorian Gray* with being an immoral tale. It also succinctly sets forth the tenets of Wilde's philosophy of art. Devoted to a school of thought and a mode of sensibility known as aestheticism, Wilde believed that art possesses an intrinsic value— that it is beautiful and therefore has worth, and thus needs serve no other purpose, be it moral or political. This attitude was revolutionary in Victorian England, where popular belief held that art was not only a function of morality but also a means of enforcing it. In the Preface, Wilde also cautioned readers against finding meanings "beneath the surface" of art. Part gothic novel, part comedy of manners, part treatise on the relationship between art and morality, *The Picture of Dorian Gray* continues to present its readers with a puzzle to sort out. There is as likely to be as much disagreement over its meaning now as there was among its Victorian audience, but, as

2 ❦ OSCAR WILDE

CONTEXT

Wilde notes near the end of the Preface, "Diversity of opinion about a work of art shows that the work is new, complex, and vital."

In 1891, the same year that the second edition of *The Picture of Dorian Gray* was published, Wilde began a homosexual relationship with Lord Alfred Douglas, an aspiring but rather untalented poet. The affair caused a good deal of scandal, and Douglas's father, the marquess of Queensberry, eventually criticized it publicly. When Wilde sued the marquess for libel, he himself was convicted under English sodomy laws for acts of "gross indecency." In 1895, Wilde was sentenced to two years of hard labor, during which time he wrote a long, heartbreaking letter to Lord Alfred titled *De Profundis* (Latin for "Out of the Depths"). After his release, Wilde left England and divided his time between France and Italy, living in poverty. He never published under his own name again, but, in 1898, he did publish under a pseudonym *The Ballad of Reading Gaol*, a lengthy poem about a prisoner's feelings toward another prisoner about to be executed. Wilde died in Paris on November 30, 1900, having converted to Roman Catholicism on his deathbed.

PLOT OVERVIEW

I N THE STATELY LONDON HOME of his aunt, Lady Brandon, the well-known artist Basil Hallward meets Dorian Gray. Dorian is a cultured, wealthy, and impossibly beautiful young man who immediately captures Basil's artistic imagination. Dorian sits for several portraits, and Basil often depicts him as an ancient Greek hero or a mythological figure. When the novel opens, the artist is completing his first portrait of Dorian as he truly is, but, as he admits to his friend Lord Henry Wotton, the painting disappoints him because it reveals too much of his feeling for his subject. Lord Henry, a famous wit who enjoys scandalizing his friends by celebrating youth, beauty, and the selfish pursuit of pleasure, disagrees, claiming that the portrait is Basil's masterpiece. Dorian arrives at the studio, and Basil reluctantly introduces him to Lord Henry, who he fears will have a damaging influence on the impressionable, young Dorian.

Basil's fears are well founded; before the end of their first conversation, Lord Henry upsets Dorian with a speech about the transient nature of beauty and youth. Worried that these, his most impressive characteristics, are fading day by day, Dorian curses his portrait, which he believes will one day remind him of the beauty he will have lost. In a fit of distress, he pledges his soul if only the painting could bear the burden of age and infamy, allowing him to stay forever young. In an attempt to appease Dorian, Basil gives him the portrait.

Over the next few weeks, Lord Henry's influence over Dorian grows stronger. The youth becomes a disciple of the "new Hedonism" and proposes to live a life dedicated to the pursuit of pleasure. He falls in love with Sibyl Vane, a young actress who performs in a theater in London's slums. He adores her acting; she, in turn, refers to him as "Prince Charming" and refuses to heed the warnings of her brother, James Vane, that Dorian is no good for her. Overcome by her emotions for Dorian, Sibyl decides that she can no longer act, wondering how she can pretend to love on the stage now that she has experienced the real thing. Dorian, who loves Sibyl *because* of her ability to act, cruelly breaks his engagement with her. After doing so, he returns home to notice that his face in Basil's portrait of him has changed: it now sneers. Frightened that his wish for his likeness in the painting to bear the ill effects of his behavior has come

3

true and that his sins will be recorded on the canvas, he resolves to make amends with Sibyl the next day. The following afternoon, however, Lord Henry brings news that Sibyl has killed herself. At Lord Henry's urging, Dorian decides to consider her death a sort of artistic triumph—she personified tragedy—and to put the matter behind him. Meanwhile, Dorian hides his portrait in a remote upper room of his house, where no one other than he can watch its transformation.

Lord Henry gives Dorian a book that describes the wicked exploits of a nineteenth-century Frenchman; it becomes Dorian's bible as he sinks ever deeper into a life of sin and corruption. He lives a life devoted to garnering new experiences and sensations with no regard for conventional standards of morality or the consequences of his actions. Eighteen years pass. Dorian's reputation suffers in circles of polite London society, where rumors spread regarding his scandalous exploits. His peers nevertheless continue to accept him because he remains young and beautiful. The figure in the painting, however, grows increasingly wizened and hideous. On a dark, foggy night, Basil Hallward arrives at Dorian's home to confront him about the rumors that plague his reputation. The two argue, and Dorian eventually offers Basil a look at his (Dorian's) soul. He shows Basil the now-hideous portrait, and Hallward, horrified, begs him to repent. Dorian claims it is too late for penance and kills Basil in a fit of rage.

In order to dispose of the body, Dorian employs the help of an estranged friend, a doctor, whom he blackmails. The night after the murder, Dorian makes his way to an opium den, where he encounters James Vane, who attempts to avenge Sibyl's death. Dorian escapes to his country estate. While entertaining guests, he notices James Vane peering in through a window, and he becomes wracked by fear and guilt. When a hunting party accidentally shoots and kills Vane, Dorian feels safe again. He resolves to amend his life but cannot muster the courage to confess his crimes, and the painting now reveals his supposed desire to repent for what it is—hypocrisy. In a fury, Dorian picks up the knife he used to stab Basil Hallward and attempts to destroy the painting. There is a crash, and his servants enter to find the portrait, unharmed, showing Dorian Gray as a beautiful young man. On the floor lies the body of their master—an old man, horribly wrinkled and disfigured, with a knife plunged into his heart.

CHARACTER LIST

Dorian Gray A radiantly handsome, impressionable, and wealthy young gentleman, whose portrait the artist Basil Hallward paints. Under the influence of Lord Henry Wotton, Dorian becomes extremely concerned with the transience of his beauty and begins to pursue his own pleasure above all else. He devotes himself to having as many experiences as possible, whether moral or immoral, elegant or sordid.

Lord Henry Wotton A nobleman and a close friend of Basil Hallward. Urbane and witty, Lord Henry is perpetually armed and ready with well-phrased epigrams criticizing the moralism and hypocrisy of Victorian society. His pleasure-seeking philosophy of "new Hedonism," which espouses garnering experiences that stimulate the senses without regard for conventional morality, plays a vital role in Dorian's development.

Basil Hallward An artist, and a friend of Lord Henry. Basil becomes obsessed with Dorian after meeting him at a party. He claims that Dorian possesses a beauty so rare that it has helped him realize a new kind of art; through Dorian, he finds "the lines of a fresh school." Dorian also helps Basil realize his artistic potential, as the portrait of Dorian that Basil paints proves to be his masterpiece.

Sibyl Vane A poor, beautiful, and talented actress with whom Dorian falls in love. Sibyl's love for Dorian compromises her ability to act, as her experience of true love in life makes her realize the falseness of affecting emotions onstage.

James Vane Sibyl's brother, a sailor bound for Australia. James cares deeply for his sister and worries about her relationship with Dorian. Distrustful of his mother's motives, he believes that Mrs. Vane's interest in Dorian's wealth disables her from properly protecting Sibyl. As a result, James is hesitant to leave his sister.

Mrs. Vane Sibyl and James's mother. Mrs. Vane is a faded actress who has consigned herself and her daughter to a tawdry theater company, the owner of which has helped her to pay her debts. She conceives of Dorian Gray as a wonderful alliance for her daughter because of his wealth; this ulterior motive, however, clouds her judgment and leaves Sibyl vulnerable.

Alan Campbell Once an intimate friend, Alan Campbell is one of many promising young men who have severed ties with Dorian because of Dorian's sullied reputation.

Lady Agatha Lord Henry's aunt. Lady Agatha is active in charity work in the London slums.

Lord Fermor Lord Henry's irascible uncle. Lord Fermor tells Henry the story of Dorian's parentage.

Duchess of Monmouth A pretty, bored young noblewoman who flirts with Dorian at his country estate.

Victoria Wotton Lord Henry's wife. Victoria appears only once in the novel, greeting Dorian as he waits for Lord Henry. She is described as an untidy, foolishly romantic woman with "a perfect mania for going to church."

Victor Dorian's servant. Although Victor is a trustworthy servant, Dorian becomes suspicious of him and sends him out on needless errands to ensure that he does not attempt to steal a glance at Dorian's portrait.

Mrs. Leaf Dorian Gray's housekeeper. Mrs. Leaf is a bustling older woman who takes her work seriously.

ANALYSIS OF MAJOR CHARACTERS

DORIAN GRAY

At the opening of the novel, Dorian Gray exists as something of an ideal: he is the archetype of male youth and beauty. As such, he captures the imagination of Basil Hallward, a painter, and Lord Henry Wotton, a nobleman who imagines fashioning the impressionable Dorian into an unremitting pleasure-seeker. Dorian is exceptionally vain and becomes convinced, in the course of a brief conversation with Lord Henry, that his most salient characteristics—his youth and physical attractiveness—are ever waning. The thought of waking one day without these attributes sends Dorian into a tailspin: he curses his fate and pledges his soul if only he could live without bearing the physical burdens of aging and sinning. He longs to be as youthful and lovely as the masterpiece that Basil has painted of him, and he wishes that the portrait could age in his stead. His vulnerability and insecurity in these moments make him excellent clay for Lord Henry's willing hands.

Dorian soon leaves Basil's studio for Lord Henry's parlor, where he adopts the tenets of "the new Hedonism" and resolves to live his life as a pleasure-seeker with no regard for conventional morality. His relationship with Sibyl Vane tests his commitment to this philosophy. his love of the young actress nearly leads him to dispense with Lord Henry's teachings, but his love proves to be as shallow as he is. When he breaks Sibyl's heart and drives her to suicide, Dorian notices the first change in his portrait—evidence that his portrait is showing the effects of age and experience while his body remains ever youthful. Dorian experiences a moment of crisis, as he weighs his guilt about his treatment of Sibyl against the freedom from worry that Lord Henry's philosophy has promised. When Dorian decides to view Sibyl's death as the achievement of an artistic ideal rather than a needless tragedy for which he is responsible, he starts down the steep and slippery slope of his own demise.

As Dorian's sins grow worse over the years, his likeness in Basil's portrait grows more hideous. Dorian seems to lack a conscience, but the desire to repent that he eventually feels illustrates that he is indeed human. Despite the beautiful things with which he surrounds himself, he is unable to distract himself from the dissipation of his soul. His murder of Basil marks the beginning of his end: although in the past he has been able to sweep infamies from his mind, he cannot shake the thought that he has killed his friend. Dorian's guilt tortures him relentlessly until he is forced to do away with his portrait. In the end, Dorian seems punished by his ability to be influenced: if the new social order celebrates individualism, as Lord Henry claims, Dorian falters because he fails to establish and live by his own moral code.

LORD HENRY WOTTON

Lord Henry is a man possessed of "wrong, fascinating, poisonous, delightful theories." He is a charming talker, a famous wit, and a brilliant intellect. Given the seductive way in which he leads conversation, it is little wonder that Dorian falls under his spell so completely. Lord Henry's theories are radical; they aim to shock and purposefully attempt to topple established, untested, or conventional notions of truth. In the end, however, they prove naïve, and Lord Henry himself fails to realize the implications of most of what he says.

Lord Henry is a relatively static character—he does not undergo a significant change in the course of the narrative. He is as coolly composed, unshakable, and possessed of the same dry wit in the final pages of the novel as he is upon his introduction. Because he does not change while Dorian and Basil clearly do, his philosophy seems amusing and enticing in the first half of the book, but improbable and shallow in the second. Lord Henry muses in Chapter Nineteen, for instance, that there are no immoral books; he claims that "[t]he books that the world calls immoral are books that show the world its own shame." But since the decadent book that Lord Henry lends Dorian facilitates Dorian's downfall, it is difficult to accept what Lord Henry says as true.

Although Lord Henry is a self-proclaimed hedonist who advocates the equal pursuit of both moral and immoral experience, he lives a rather staid life. He participates in polite London society and attends parties and the theater, but he does not indulge in sordid behavior. Unlike Dorian, he does not lead innocent youths to suicide or travel incognito to the city's most despised and desperate quarters. Lord Henry thus has little notion of the practical effects of his philosophy. His claim that Dorian could never commit a murder because "[c]rime belongs exclusively to the lower orders" demonstrates the limitations of his understanding of the human soul. It is not surprising, then, that he fails to appreciate the profound meaning of Dorian's downfall.

BASIL HALLWARD

Basil Hallward is a talented, though somewhat conventionally minded, painter. His love for Dorian Gray, which seems to reflect Oscar Wilde's own affection for his young lover, Lord Alfred Douglas, changes the way he sees art; indeed, it defines a new school of expression for him. Basil's portrait of Dorian marks a new phase of his career. Before he created this masterwork, he spent his time painting Dorian in the veils of antiquity—dressed as an ancient soldier or as various romantic figures from mythology. Once he has painted Dorian as he truly is, however, he fears that he has put too much of himself into the work. He worries that his love, which he himself describes as "idolatry," is too apparent, and that it betrays too much of himself. Though he later changes his mind to believe that art is always more abstract than one thinks and that the painting thus betrays nothing except form and color, his emotional investment in Dorian remains constant. He seeks to protect Dorian, voicing his objection to Lord Henry's injurious influence over Dorian and defending Dorian even after their relationship has clearly dissolved. Basil's commitment to Dorian, which ultimately proves fatal, reveals the genuineness of his love for his favorite subject and his concern for the safety and salvation of Dorian's soul.

THEMES, MOTIFS & SYMBOLS

THEMES

Themes are the fundamental and often universal ideas explored in a literary work.

THE PURPOSE OF ART

When *The Picture of Dorian Gray* was first published in *Lippincott's Monthly Magazine* in 1890, it was decried as immoral. In revising the text the following year, Wilde included a preface, which serves as a useful explanation of his philosophy of art. The purpose of art, according to this series of epigrams, is to have no purpose. In order to understand this claim fully, one needs to consider the moral climate of Wilde's time and the Victorian sensibility regarding art and morality. The Victorians believed that art could be used as a tool for social education and moral enlightenment, as illustrated in works by writers such as Charles Dickens and George Gissing. The aestheticism movement, of which Wilde was a major proponent, sought to free art from this responsibility. The aestheticists were motivated as much by a contempt for bourgeois morality—a sensibility embodied in *Dorian Gray* by Lord Henry, whose every word seems designed to shock the ethical certainties of the burgeoning middle class—as they were by the belief that art need not possess any other purpose than being beautiful.

If this philosophy informed Wilde's life, we must then consider whether his only novel bears it out. The two works of art that dominate the novel—Basil's painting and the mysterious yellow book that Lord Henry gives Dorian—are presented in the vein more of Victorian sensibilities than of aesthetic ones. That is, both the portrait and the French novel serve a purpose: the first acts as a type of mysterious mirror that shows Dorian the physical dissipation his own body has been spared, while the second acts as something of a road map, leading the young man farther along the path toward infamy. While we know nothing of the circumstances of the yellow book's composition, Basil's state of mind while painting Dorian's portrait is clear. Later in the novel, he advocates that all art be "unconscious, ideal, and remote." His portrait of Dorian, however, is anything but. Thus, Basil's initial refusal to exhibit the work results from his belief that it betrays his idolization of his subject. Of course, one might consider that these breaches of aesthetic philosophy mold *The Picture of Dorian Gray* into something of a cautionary tale: these are the prices that must be paid for insisting that art reveals the artist or a moral lesson. But this warning is, in itself, a moral lesson, which perhaps betrays the impossibility of Wilde's project. If, as Dorian observes late in the novel, the imagination orders the chaos of life and invests it with meaning, then art, as the fruit of the imagination, cannot help but mean something. Wilde may have succeeded in freeing his art from the confines of Victorian morality, but he has replaced it with a doctrine that is, in its own way, just as restrictive.

THE SUPREMACY OF YOUTH AND BEAUTY

The first principle of aestheticism, the philosophy of art by which Oscar Wilde lived, is that art serves no other purpose than to offer beauty. Throughout *The Picture of Dorian Gray*, beauty reigns. It is a means to revitalize the wearied senses, as indicated by the effect that Basil's painting has on the cynical Lord Henry. It is also a means of escaping the brutalities of the world: Dorian distances himself, not to mention his consciousness, from the horrors of his actions by devoting himself to the study of beautiful things—music, jewels, rare tapestries. In a society that prizes beauty so highly, youth and physical attractiveness become valuable commodities. Lord Henry reminds Dorian of as much upon their first meeting, when he laments that Dorian will soon enough lose his most precious attributes. In Chapter Seventeen, the Duchess of Monmouth suggests to Lord Henry that he places too much value on these things; indeed, Dorian's eventual demise confirms her suspicions. For although beauty and youth remain of utmost importance at the end of the novel—the portrait is, after all, returned to its original form—the novel suggests that the price one must pay for them is exceedingly high. Indeed, Dorian gives nothing less than his soul.

THE SUPERFICIAL NATURE OF SOCIETY

It is no surprise that a society that prizes beauty above all else is a society founded on a love of surfaces. What matters most to Dorian, Lord Henry, and the polite company they keep is not whether a man is good at heart but rather whether he is handsome. As Dorian evolves into the realization of a type, the perfect blend of scholar and socialite, he experiences the freedom to abandon his morals without censure. Indeed, even though, as Basil warns, society's elite question his name and reputation, Dorian is never ostracized. On the contrary, despite his "mode of life," he remains at the heart of the London social scene because of the "innocence" and "purity of his face." As Lady Narborough notes to Dorian, there is little (if any) distinction between ethics and appearance: "you are made to be good—you look so good."

THE NEGATIVE CONSEQUENCES OF INFLUENCE

The painting and the yellow book have a profound effect on Dorian, influencing him to predominantly immoral behavior over the course of nearly two decades. Reflecting on Dorian's power over Basil and deciding that he would like to seduce Dorian in much the same way, Lord Henry points out that there is "something terribly enthralling in the exercise of influence." Falling under the sway of such influence is, perhaps, unavoidable, but the novel ultimately censures the sacrifice of one's self to another. Basil's idolatry of Dorian leads to his murder, and Dorian's devotion to Lord Henry's hedonism and the yellow book precipitate his own downfall. It is little wonder, in a novel that prizes individualism—the uncompromised expression of self—that the sacrifice of one's self, whether it be to another person or to a work of art, leads to one's destruction.

MOTIFS

Motifs are recurring structures, contrasts, or literary devices that can help to develop and inform the text's major themes.

THE PICTURE OF DORIAN GRAY

The picture of Dorian Gray, "the most magical of mirrors," shows Dorian the physical burdens of age and sin from which he has been spared. For a time, Dorian sets his conscience aside and lives his life according to a single goal: achieving pleasure. His painted image, however, asserts itself as his conscience and hounds him with the knowledge of his crimes: there he sees the cruelty he showed to Sibyl Vane and the blood he spilled killing Basil Hallward.

HOMOEROTIC MALE RELATIONSHIPS

The homoerotic bonds between men play a large role in structuring the novel. Basil's painting depends upon his adoration of Dorian's beauty; similarly, Lord Henry is overcome with the desire to seduce Dorian and mold him into the realization of a type. This camaraderie between men fits into Wilde's larger aesthetic values, for it returns him to antiquity, where an appreciation of youth and beauty was not only fundamental to culture but was also expressed as a physical relationship between men. As a homosexual living in an intolerant society, Wilde asserted this philosophy partially in an attempt to justify his own lifestyle. For Wilde, homosexuality was not a sordid vice but rather a sign of refined culture. As he claimed rather romantically during his trial for "gross indecency" between men, the affection between an older and younger man places one in the tradition of Plato, Michelangelo, and Shakespeare.

THE COLOR WHITE

Interestingly, Dorian's trajectory from figure of innocence to figure of degradation can be charted by Wilde's use of the color white. White usually connotes innocence and blankness, as it does when Dorian is first introduced. It is, in fact, "the white purity" of Dorian's boyhood that Lord Henry finds so captivating. Basil invokes whiteness when he learns that Dorian has sacrificed his innocence, and, as the artist stares in horror at the ruined portrait, he quotes a biblical verse from the Book of Isaiah: "Though your sins be as scarlet, yet I will make them as white as snow." But the days of Dorian's innocence are over. It is a quality he now eschews, and, tellingly, when he orders flowers, he demands "as few white ones as possible." When the color appears again, in the form of James Vane's face—"like a white handkerchief"—peering in through a window, it has been transformed from the color of innocence to the color of death. It is this threatening pall that makes Dorian long, at the novel's end, for his "rose-white boyhood," but the hope is in vain, and he proves unable to wash away the stains of his sins.

SYMBOLS

Symbols are objects, characters, figures, or colors used to represent abstract ideas or concepts.

THE OPIUM DENS

The opium dens, located in a remote and derelict section of London, represent the sordid state of Dorian's mind. He flees to them at a crucial moment. After killing Basil, Dorian seeks to forget the awfulness of his crimes by losing consciousness in a drug-induced stupor. Although he has a canister of opium in his home, he leaves the safety of his neat and proper parlor to travel to the dark dens that reflect the degradation of his soul.

JAMES VANE

James Vane is less a believable character than an embodiment of Dorian's tortured conscience. As Sibyl's brother, he is a rather flat caricature of the avenging relative. Still, Wilde saw him as essential to the story, adding his character during his revision of 1891. Appearing at the dock and later at Dorian's country estate, James has an almost spectral quality. Like the ghost of Jacob Marley in Charles Dickens's *A Christmas Carol,* who warns Scrooge of the sins he will have to face, James appears with his face "like a white handkerchief" to goad Dorian into accepting responsibility for the crimes he has committed.

THE YELLOW BOOK

Lord Henry gives Dorian a copy of the yellow book as a gift. Although he never gives the title, Wilde describes the book as a French novel that charts the outrageous experiences of its pleasure-seeking protagonist (we can fairly assume that the book in question is Joris-Karl Huysman's decadent nineteenth-century novel *À Rebours,* translated as "Against the Grain" or "Against Nature"). The book becomes like holy scripture to Dorian, who buys nearly a dozen copies and bases his life and actions on it. The book represents the profound and damaging influence that art can have over an individual and serves as a warning to those who would surrender themselves so completely to such an influence.

SYMBOLS

Summary & Analysis

The Preface–Chapter Two

> *We are punished for our refusals. Every impulse that we strive to strangle broods in the mind, and poisons us.*
> *(See* Quotations, *p. 47)*

Summary: The Preface

The Preface is a series of epigrams, or concise, witty sayings, that express the major points of Oscar Wilde's aesthetic philosophy. In short, the epigrams praise beauty and repudiate the notion that art serves a moral purpose.

Summary: Chapter One

The novel begins in the elegantly appointed London home of Basil Hallward, a well-known artist. Basil discusses his latest portrait with his friend, the clever and scandalously amoral Lord Henry Wotton. Lord Henry admires the painting, the subject of which is a gorgeous, golden-haired young man. Believing it to be Basil's finest work, he insists that the painter exhibit it. Basil, however, refuses, claiming that he cannot show the work in public because he has put too much of himself into it. When Lord Henry presses him for a more satisfying reason, Basil reluctantly describes how he met his young subject, whose name is Dorian Gray, at a party. He admits that, upon seeing Dorian for the first time, he was terrified; indeed, he was overcome by the feeling that his life was "on the verge of a terrible crisis." Dorian has become, however, an object of fascination and obsession for Basil, who sees the young man every day and declares him to be his sole inspiration. Basil admits that he cannot bring himself to exhibit the portrait because the piece betrays the "curious artistic idolatry" that Dorian inspires in him.

Lord Henry, astonished by this declaration, remembers where he heard the name Dorian Gray before: his aunt, Lady Agatha, mentioned that the young man promised to help her with charity work in the slums of London. At that moment, the butler announces that Dorian Gray has arrived, and Lord Henry insists on meeting him. Basil reluctantly agrees but begs his friend not to try to influence the young man. According to Basil, Dorian has a "simple and a beautiful nature" that could easily be spoiled by Lord Henry's cynicism.

SUMMARY: CHAPTER TWO

Dorian Gray proves to be every bit as a handsome as his portrait. Basil introduces him to Lord Henry, and Dorian begs Lord Henry to stay and talk to him while he sits for Basil. Basil warns Dorian that Lord Henry is a bad influence, and Dorian seems intrigued by this idea. Lord Henry agrees to stay and, while Basil puts the finishing touches on the portrait, discusses his personal philosophy, which holds that "the highest of all duties [is] the duty that one owes to one's self." While Basil continues to work, Lord Henry escorts Dorian into the garden, where he praises Dorian's youth and beauty and warns him how surely and quickly those qualities will fade. He urges Dorian to live life to its fullest, to spend his time "always searching for new sensations" rather than devoting himself to "common" or "vulgar" pastimes.

Basil calls the men inside, and Dorian sits for another quarter of an hour until the portrait is complete. It is a thing of remarkable beauty—"the finest portrait of modern times," Lord Henry tells Basil—but looking at it makes Dorian unhappy. Remembering Lord Henry's warning about the advance of age, he reflects that his portrait will remain young even as he himself grows old and wrinkled. He curses this fate and pledges his soul "[i]f it were only the other way." Basil tries to comfort the young man, but Dorian pushes him away. Declaring that he will not allow the painting to ruin their friendship, Basil makes a move to destroy it. Dorian stops him, saying that he loves the painting, and a relieved Basil promises to give it to him as a gift. Dorian and Lord Henry depart after Dorian promises, despite Basil's objections, to go to the theater with Lord Henry later that evening.

ANALYSIS: THE PREFACE–CHAPTER TWO

The Preface to *The Picture of Dorian Gray* is a collection of epigrams that aptly sums up the philosophical tenets of the artistic and philosophical movement known as aestheticism. Aestheticism, which found its footing in Europe in the early nineteenth century, proposed that art need not serve moral, political, or otherwise didactic ends. Whereas the romantic movement of the early and mid-nineteenth century viewed art as a product of the human creative impulse that could be used to learn more about humankind and the world, the aesthetic movement denied that art must necessarily be an instructive force in order to be valuable. Instead, the aestheticists believed, art should be valuable in and of itself—*art for art's sake.* Near the end of the nineteenth century, Walter Pater, an English essayist and critic, suggested that life itself should be lived in the spirit of art. His views, especially those presented in a collection of essays called *The Renaissance,* had a profound impact on the English poets of the 1890s, most notably Oscar Wilde.

Aestheticism flourished partly as a reaction against the materialism of the burgeoning middle class, assumed to be composed of philistines (individuals ignorant of art) who responded to art in a generally unrefined manner. In this climate, the artist could assert him- or herself as a remarkable and rarefied being, one leading the search for beauty in an age marked by shameful class inequality, social hypocrisy, and bourgeois complacency. No one latched onto this attitude more boldly, or with more flair, than Oscar Wilde. His determination to live a life of beauty and to mold his life into a work of art is reflected in the beliefs and actions of several characters in Wilde's only novel.

The Picture of Dorian Gray has often been compared to the famous German legend of Faust, immortalized in Christopher Marlowe's sixteenth-century play *Doctor Faustus* and in Johann Wolfgang von Goethe's nineteenth-century poem *Faust.* The legend tells of a learned doctor who sells his soul to the devil in return for knowledge and magical abilities. Although Dorian Gray never contracts with the devil, his sacrifice is similar: he trades his soul for the luxury of eternal youth. For its overtones of supernaturalism, its refusal to satisfy popular morality, and its portrayal of homoerotic culture, *The Picture of Dorian Gray* was met with harsh criticism. Many considered the novel dangerously subversive, one offended critic calling it "a poisonous book, the atmosphere of which is heavy with the mephitic odours of moral and spiritual putrefaction."

The fear of a bad—or good—influence is, in fact, one of the novel's primary concerns. As a work that sets forth a philosophy of aestheticism, the novel questions the degree and kind of influence a work of art can have over an individual. Furthermore, since the novel conceives of art as including a well-lived life, it is also interested in the kind of influence one person can have over another. After all, the artful Lord Henry himself has as profound an effect upon Dorian's life as Basil's painting does.

While Lord Henry exercises influence over other characters primarily through his skillful use of language, it is Dorian's beauty that seduces the characters with whom he associates. Basil, a serious artist and rather dull moralist, admits that Dorian has had "[s]ome subtle influence" over him; it is this influence that Basil is certain that his painting reveals. As he confides to Lord Henry, "I have put into it some expression of all this curious artistic idolatry." Ultimately, however, Lord Henry's brilliant speech is a much more influential force than aesthetic beauty. His witty and biting epigrams threaten to seduce not only the impressionable young Dorian but the reader as well. Lord Henry's ironic speech cuts through social convention and hypocrisy to reveal unexpected, unpleasant truths.

The characters whose lifestyles Lord Henry criticizes resist his extreme theories. Basil's resistance to Lord Henry's argument that scandal is a function of class typifies the reactions of the characters whom Lord Henry criticizes; after all, their position and comfort depend upon the hypocrisies he tends to expose. To some degree, every character in the novel is seduced by Lord Henry's philosophies, Dorian Gray more so than anyone else. In these opening chapters, Dorian emerges as an incredibly impressionable young man, someone who Basil fears is open to the "influence" of Lord Henry, which will "spoil" him. Basil's fear is well founded, as before the end of his first conversation with Lord Henry, Dorian is "dimly conscious that entirely fresh influences were at work within him."

CHAPTERS THREE–FOUR

SUMMARY: CHAPTER THREE

Shortly after his first meeting with Dorian Gray, Lord Henry visits his uncle, Lord Fermor, a "genial if somewhat rough-mannered" old nobleman. When Lord Henry asks his uncle about Dorian Gray's past, the old man tells him that Dorian comes from an unhappy family with a dark, tangled history. He relates that Dorian's mother, a noblewoman, eloped with a poor soldier; the woman's father, a villainous old lord, arranged to have his daughter's husband killed just before Dorian was born. The grieving widow died soon thereafter, leaving Dorian to be raised by a loveless tyrant. With this information, Lord Henry becomes increasingly fascinated with Dorian; he finds the story romantic and delights in the thought that he might influence the young man, making "that wonderful spirit his own."

Shortly thereafter, Lord Henry goes to dine at the home of his aunt, Lady Agatha, where several of London's elite upper class—Dorian included—have gathered. Lord Henry scandalizes the group by going on at length about the virtues of hedonism and selfishness and mocking his aunt's philanthropic efforts. "I can sympathize with everything," he remarks at one point, "except suffering." He insists that one's life should be spent appreciating beauty and seeking out pleasure rather than searching for ways to alleviate pain and tragedy. Many of the guests are appalled by his selfishness, but he is so clever and witty that they are charmed in spite of themselves. Dorian Gray is particularly fascinated, so much so that he leaves with Lord Henry and abandons his earlier plans to visit Basil.

SUMMARY: CHAPTER FOUR

One month later, while waiting in Lord Henry's home for his host to arrive, Dorian discusses music with Lord Henry's wife, Victoria. When Lord Henry arrives, Dorian rushes to him, eager to share the news that he has fallen in love. The girl, he reports, is Sibyl Vane, an actress who plays Shakespeare's heroines in repertoire in a cheap London theater. Dorian admits to discovering her while wandering through the slums: inspired by Lord Henry's advice to "know everything about life," he had entered a playhouse. Despite the tawdriness of the locale and his disdain for the theater owner, Dorian decided that the star, Sibyl Vane, was the finest actress he had ever seen. After several trips to the theater, the owner insisted that Dorian meet Ms. Vane, who, awed by the attentions of such a handsome gentleman, declared that she would refer to him as "Prince Charming." Lord Henry, amused by this development, agrees to accompany Dorian to see Sibyl Vane play the lead in *Romeo and Juliet* the following night. Basil is to join them, and Dorian remarks that Basil sent him his portrait, framed, a few days earlier.

After Dorian leaves, Lord Henry muses on his influence over the young man, reflecting on how fascinating the psychology of another human being can be. He then dresses and goes out to dinner. He comes home late that night and finds a telegram from Dorian waiting for him. It states that he is engaged to be married to Sibyl Vane.

ANALYSIS: CHAPTERS THREE–FOUR

The Picture of Dorian Gray is a curious mixture of different genres. It displays Wilde's incomparable talent for social comedy and satire, even as it veers toward the formula for Gothic literature. Gothic fiction, which was tremendously popular in the late eighteenth and early nineteenth centuries, focused on tales of romance, cruelty, and horror. By the end of the nineteenth century, the formula had changed considerably, but these basic tenets remained intact. Dorian's mysterious and melodramatic heritage alludes to conventions of the Gothic novel: his wicked grandfather, his parents' cursed elopement, his father's murder, and his mother's early death represent a type of moody romance popular among Gothic authors. As the critic Donald Lawler points out, Dorian's ancestry is identical to that of the main characters in three of Wilde's short stories.

The first two chapters of the novel show Lord Henry's powers of seduction, but in Chapters Three and Four Lord Henry himself is seduced. Strictly speaking, it is not a person who draws Lord Henry in, but the possibility of having a profound effect on a person, namely Dorian: "there was something terribly enthralling in the exercise of influence." To project his soul onto Dorian and seize his spirit just as Dorian has seized Basil's imagination becomes Lord Henry's greatest desire. In Lord Henry's mind, life and art are not only connected but interchangeable. By molding Dorian into "a marvellous type" of boy, Lord Henry believes that he is countering the effects of "an age so limited and vulgar" as his own. He imagines that he will take his place among such masters as the great Italian artist Michelangelo, with whom he shares the imperative to create something of beauty. The fact that Lord Henry considers the life of another human being a viable medium for artistic expression indicates "[t]he new manner in art" that Wilde so tirelessly advocated. Indeed, many readers might find Lord Henry heartless, given his willingness to watch Dorian's development with practically no thought of consequence. After all, Dorian's beauty is all that matters to him, and "[i]t was no matter [to Lord Henry] how it all ended, or was destined to end." This behavior merely links Lord Henry to the tenets of aestheticism, whereby beauty is of primary importance, and vice and virtue—as Wilde states in the novel's preface—are nothing more than "materials for an art."

If the opening chapters position the three main characters in a triangular relationship, wherein Lord Henry and Basil vie for Dorian's soul and affections, Lord Henry quickly wins at the end of Chapter Three. In Dorian's declaration that he will miss his appointment with Basil in order to hear Lord Henry speak, we see that Lord Henry's hopes to dominate and influence the young man have more or less been fulfilled. Dorian gives his affections over largely because of Lord Henry's conversational skill; he asks Lord Henry to "promise to talk to me all the time." Indeed, Lord Henry is a great talker, a wonderful philosopher of "the new Hedonism," but, unlike Dorian, he acts on nothing that would damage his respectable reputation or life.

CHAPTERS FIVE–SIX

Modern morality consists in accepting the standard of one's age. I consider that for any man of culture to accept the standard of his age is a form of the grossest immorality.   (See QUOTATIONS, *p. 48*)

SUMMARY: CHAPTER FIVE

At the Vane household, Sibyl Vane is deliriously happy over her romance with Dorian Gray. Mrs. Vane, her mother, is less enthusiastic, and she alternately worries over Dorian's intentions and hopes that her daughter will benefit from his obvious wealth. Sibyl's brother, James, is also rather cautious regarding the match. As a sailor preparing to depart for Australia, James arrives to say his good-byes and warns his mother that she must watch over Sibyl. Mrs. Vane assures him that admirers such as Dorian Gray are not uncommon to actresses, and that there is no reason not to "contract an alliance" with one so wealthy. Impatient with his mother's "affectations," James takes Sibyl on a walk. Rather than discuss her Prince Charming, Sibyl chatters on about the adventures James is certain to find in Australia. She imagines him discovering gold but then, thinking this life too dangerous, states that he will be better off as a quiet sheep farmer.

James cannot shake the feeling that he is leaving his sister at an inopportune time. He doubts both Dorian's intentions and his mother's ability to protect Sibyl from them. Finally, James asks Sibyl about her suitor. He warns her against Dorian, and Sibyl carries on about the ecstasy of her new love. As the two sit and watch "the smart people go by," Sibyl sees Dorian pass in an open carriage. She points him out, but he is gone before James sees him. James swears fiercely that if Dorian ever wrongs her, he will track down her "Prince Charming" and kill him. Sibyl pledges undying devotion to Dorian. Later that night, James confronts his mother, asking her whether she was ever married to his father. Mrs. Vane answers no, and James begs her not to let Sibyl meet the same fate. Before departing, James again pledges to kill Dorian should Sibyl ever come to harm by him.

SUMMARY: CHAPTER SIX

That evening over dinner, Lord Henry announces to Basil Dorian's plan to marry Sibyl. Basil expresses concern that Dorian has decided to marry so far beneath his social position. Lord Henry claims that he himself cannot pass such judgment and that he is simply interested in observing the boy and his experiences, regardless of the outcome. Basil doubts that Lord Henry would be so cavalier if Dorian's life was, in fact, "spoiled," but Lord Henry insists that "no life is spoiled but one whose growth is arrested."

Dorian enters, and he relates the story of his engagement, which was precipitated by his seeing Sibyl play the Shakespearean heroine Rosalind (in *As You Like It*). Dorian, in a state of tremendous excitement, remarks that his love for Sibyl and his desire to live only for her have shown him the falsehood of all of Lord Henry's seductive theories about the virtues of selfishness. Lord Henry, by no means discouraged by Dorian's speech, defends his point of view by claiming that it is nature, not he, who dictates the pursuit of pleasure. The three men make their way to a theater in the slums where Sibyl Vane is to perform that night.

ANALYSIS: CHAPTERS FIVE–SIX

Critical reception of *The Picture of Dorian Gray* was mixed, with many readers condemning the novel as decadent or unmanly. The relationship between Lord Henry and Dorian, as well the one of Basil and Dorian, is clearly homoerotic, and must have shocked readers who valued Victorian respectability. Although Wilde stops short of stating that Basil and Lord Henry have sexual feelings for Dorian, the language he uses to describe their devotion to Dorian is unmistakably the language of deep, romantic intimacy. Wilde's language of irony facilitates dodging direct statements; in one scene, for example, although the ostensible topic of conversation is Dorian as a subject for portraits, the exchange between Basil and Lord Henry betrays the romantic nature of Basil's feelings:

> [Lord Henry:] "Tell me more about Mr Dorian Gray. How often do you see him?"
> [Basil Hallward:] "Every day. I couldn't be happy if I didn't see him everyday. He is absolutely necessary to me."

Men do have relationships with women in the novel—Dorian falls in love with Sibyl and Lord Henry himself is married—but the novel's heterosexual relationships prove to be rather superficial and short-lived. If the novel is homoerotic, it is also misogynistic. Victoria Wotton, like most of the women in the novel, is depicted with no real depth: she is briefly (and not kindly) introduced, never to be heard from again. The most significant female character in the novel is Sibyl, who seems to fulfill Lord Henry's observation that "[w]omen are a decorative sex." There is precious little substance to Sibyl's character, as becomes clear in following chapters when she so easily gives up her greatest talent in order to pursue a relationship with Dorian. In this section, as she strolls through the park with James, she emerges as a rather foolishly romantic young woman. She is perfectly content to fall in love with a stranger whom she knows only by the fairy-tale name with which she has christened him. Indeed, Sibyl is little more than a placeholder in a prefabricated romance. Dorian says nearly as much when he describes the thrill of seeing her placed "on a pedestal of gold . . . to see the world worship the woman who is mine." This sentiment confirms Lord Henry's ego-driven philosophy of women as ornaments as well as the male-centered focus of Wilde's narrative gaze: men—particularly their relationships and the influence they bring to bear upon one another—matter most in *The Picture of Dorian Gray*.

More important than Lord Henry's philosophy of the role of women, however, is his insistence on the necessity of individualism. As a mode of thinking, individualism took center stage during the nineteenth century. It was first celebrated by the Romantics, who, in the early 1800s, decided that free and spontaneous expression of the self was the true source of art and literature. The Romantics rejected the eighteenth-century sensibility that sought to imitate and reproduce the classical models of ancient Greece and Rome, which were perceived as too stylized to allow for the expression of anything genuine or relevant. Holding the self as the center of creation, Romanticism inevitably emphasized personal freedom, sensory experience, and the special status of the artist. By the time Wilde wrote *The Picture of Dorian Gray,* however, the romantic belief that man could realize these things in himself by returning to nature had largely faded. Indeed, Wilde's novel marks an interesting shift in the changing philosophy of the times. For although the residue of the Romantic movement can be seen in Dorian's story—Lord Henry advocates that nothing should hinder the freedom of the artistic individual's development—the means by which that development occurs in the story is noticeably different. In the world of *The Picture of Dorian Gray,* art is to be made by submerging oneself in society rather than escaping from it.

CHAPTERS SEVEN–EIGHT

SUMMARY: CHAPTER SEVEN

The theater is crowded when the men arrive. Dorian continues to wax eloquent about Sibyl's beauty, and Basil assures Dorian that he will support the marriage wholeheartedly since Dorian is so obviously in love. When the play begins, however, Sibyl is terrible, and her acting only worsens as the evening wears on. Unable to understand the change that has come over his beloved, Dorian is heartbroken. Basil and Lord Henry leave him, and he makes his way backstage to find Sibyl, who is quite happy despite her dreadful performance. She explains that before she met Dorian and experienced true love, she was able to inhabit other characters and feel their emotions easily, which made possible her success as an actress. Now, however, these pretend emotions no longer interest her, since they pale in relation to her real feelings for Dorian. She realizes that "the words I had to speak were unreal, were not my words, were not what I wanted to say." As a result, she declares that her career on the stage is over. Dorian, horrified by this decision, realizes that he was in love not with her but with her acting. He spurns her cruelly and tells her that he wishes never to see her again.

After a night spent wandering the streets of London, Dorian returns to his home. There, he looks at Basil's portrait of him and notices the painting has changed—a faint sneer has appeared at the corner of his likeness's mouth. He is astonished. Remembering his wish that the painting would bear the burden and marks of age and lifestyle for him, Dorian is suddenly overcome with shame about his behavior toward Sibyl. He pulls a screen in front of the portrait and goes to bed, resolving to make amends with Sibyl in the morning.

SUMMARY: CHAPTER EIGHT

Dorian does not awake until well after noon the next day. When he gets up, he goes to check the painting. In the light, the change is unmistakable; the face in the portrait has become crueler. While the stunned Dorian tries to come up with some rational explanation for the change, Lord Henry arrives with terrible news: Sibyl committed suicide the previous night. Dorian is stunned, but Lord Henry manages to convince him that he should not go to the police and explain his part in the girl's death. Lord Henry urges Dorian not to wallow in guilt but, rather, to regard Sibyl's suicide as a perfect artistic representation of undying love and appreciate it as such. Dorian, who feels numb rather than anguished, is convinced by his friend's seductive words and agrees to go to the opera with him that very night. When Lord Henry is gone, Dorian reflects that this incident is a turning point in his existence, and he resolves to accept a life of "[e]ternal youth, infinite passion, pleasures subtle and secret, wild joy and wilder sins," in which his portrait, rather than his own body, will bear the marks of age and experience. Having made this resolution, he joins Lord Henry at the opera.

ANALYSIS: CHAPTERS SEVEN–EIGHT

Dorian's romance with Sibyl represents the possibility that he will not accept Lord Henry's philosophy and will instead learn to prize human beings and emotions over art. His love for her allows him to resist Lord Henry's seductive words, noting to Lord Henry, "When I am with her, I regret all that you have taught me. . . . [T]he mere touch of Sibyl Vane's hand makes me forget you and all your wrong, fascinating, poisonous, delightful theories." But just as Lord Henry appreciates Dorian as a work of art rather than as a human being, what Dorian values most about Sibyl is her talent as an actress—her ability to portray an ideal, not her true self. The extent of Lord Henry's influence is painfully clear as Dorian heartlessly snubs Sibyl, who claims that her real love for him prohibits her from acting out such emotions onstage. Surely, to modern readers, Sibyl's devotion to Dorian—

not to mention her grief over losing him—seems a bit melodramatic. She is a rather thinly drawn character, but she serves two important functions. First, she forces us to question what precisely art is and when its effects are good. Second, she shows the pernicious consequences of a philosophy that places beauty and self-pleasure above consideration for others. Sibyl's tragic fate enables us to be as critical of Wilde's philosophies as he himself was at the end of his life.

Sibyl's claim that Dorian gives her "something higher, something of which all art is but a reflection" stands in undeniable contrast to Lord Henry's philosophy, in which art is the highest experience and life imitates art rather than vice versa. Indeed, time and again, Lord Henry delights in ignoring the significance of human emotions. Even though Sibyl's conception of art as a reflection of grand emotions counters Lord Henry's (and Wilde's) philosophy of art, it resonates throughout the remainder of the novel. Indeed, Sibyl's philosophy is echoed in the very portrait of Dorian, since it is a reflection of Dorian's true self.

The answer to the narrator's question as to whether the changing portrait "[w]ould ... teach [Dorian] to loathe his own soul" is yes, as Dorian grows increasingly uncomfortable over the course of the novel with what the disfigured portrait signifies about himself. As the novel progresses and the painting continues to register the effects of time and dissipation, we see the degree to which Dorian is undone by the sins that his portrait reflects and the degree to which he suffers for allowing the painting to act as a "visible emblem of conscience." The aging of Dorian's likeness in the portrait ultimately contradicts some of Lord Henry's—and Wilde's—beliefs about art: the painting does *not* exist in a moral vacuum. Instead, the painting both shows the deleterious effects of sin and gives Dorian a sense of freedom from morality; it thus influences and is influenced by morality.

CHAPTERS NINE–TEN

> Yes: there was to be . . . a new Hedonism that was to re-
> create life, and to save it from that harsh,
> uncomely puritanism. . . .   (See QUOTATIONS, p. 49)

SUMMARY: CHAPTER NINE

The next day, Basil comes to offer his condolences to Dorian, but Dorian dismisses the memory of Sibyl lightly and easily, remarking, "What is done is done. What is past is past." Horrified at the change in Dorian, Basil blames Lord Henry for Dorian's heartless attitude. Indeed, in discussing Sibyl's death, Dorian uses many of the same phrases and arguments that Lord Henry favors and evokes a similar air of unaffected composure. He claims that Sibyl's death elevates her "into the sphere of art." Dorian asks Basil to do a drawing of Sibyl so that he has something by which to remember her. Basil agrees and begs Dorian to return to his studio for a sitting. When Dorian refuses, Basil asks if he is displeased with his portrait, which Basil means to show at an exhibition. When Basil goes to remove the screen with which Dorian has covered the painting, Dorian's composure cracks. Dorian insists that the work never appear in public and pledges never to speak to Basil again should he touch the screen. Remembering Basil's original refusal to show the painting, Dorian asks why he has changed his mind. Basil confesses that he was worried that the painting would reveal his obsession with Dorian. Now, however, Basil believes that the painting, like all art, "conceals the artist far more completely than it ever reveals him." Basil again asks Dorian to sit for him, and Dorian again refuses. When Basil leaves, Dorian decides to hide his portrait.

SUMMARY: CHAPTER TEN

Once Basil is gone, Dorian orders his servant, Victor, to go to a nearby frame-maker and bring back two men. He then calls his housekeeper, Mrs. Leaf, whom he asks for the key to the school-room, which sits at the top of the house and has been unused for nearly five years. Dorian covers the portrait with an ornate satin coverlet, reflecting that the sins he commits will mar its beauty just as worms mar the body of a corpse. The men from the frame-maker's arrive, and Dorian employs them to carry the painting to the schoolroom. Here, Dorian muses, the painting will be safe from prying eyes, and if no one can actually see his deterioration, then it bears no importance. After locking the room, he returns to his study and settles down to read a book that Lord Henry has sent him. This yellow book is accompanied by a newspaper account of Sibyl's death. Horrified by the ugliness of the report, Dorian turns to the book, which traces the life of a young Parisian who devotes his life to "all the passions and modes of thought that belonged to every century except his own." After reading a few pages, Dorian becomes entranced. He finds the work to be "a poisonous book," one that confuses the boundaries between vice and virtue. When Dorian meets Lord Henry for dinner later that evening, he pronounces the work fascinating.

> Is insincerity such a terrible thing? I think not. It is
> merely a method by which we can multiply our
> personalities.   (See QUOTATIONS, p. 50)

ANALYSIS: CHAPTERS NINE–TEN

Sibyl's death compels Dorian to make the conscious decision to embrace Lord Henry's philosophy of selfishness and hedonism wholeheartedly. The contrast between Dorian's and Basil's reactions to Sibyl's death demonstrates the degree to which Lord Henry has changed Dorian. Dorian dismisses the need for grief in words that echo Lord Henry's: Sibyl need not be mourned, he proclaims, for she has "passed . . . into the sphere of art." In other words, Dorian thinks of Sibyl's death as he would the death of a character in a novel or painting, and chooses not to be affected emotionally by her passing. This attitude reveals one way in which the novel blurs the distinction between life and art. Dorian himself passes "into the sphere of art" when his portrait reflects the physical manifestations of age and sin. While it is usually paintings that never age and people who do, it is the other way around with Dorian, as he has become more like a work of art than a human.

Basil's declaration of his obsession with Dorian is in many ways a defense and justification of homosexual love. In 1895, five years after *Dorian Gray* was published, Wilde was famously convicted of sodomy for his romantic relationship with Lord Alfred Douglas. Wilde defended homosexual love as an emotion experienced by some of the world's greatest men. He insisted that it had its roots in ancient Greece and was, therefore, fundamental to the development

THE PICTURE OF DORIAN GRAY 🌿 31

of Western thought and culture. In his trial, when asked to describe the "love that dare not speak its name," Wilde explained it as

> such a great affection of an elder for a younger man as there was between David and Jonathan, such as Plato made the very basis of his philosophy, and such as you find in the sonnets of Michelangelo and Shakespeare. . . . It is beautiful, it is fine, it is the noblest form of affection. There is nothing unnatural about it.

This testimony is strikingly similar to Dorian's reflection upon the kind of affection that Basil shows him:

> [I]t was really love—[it] had nothing in it that was not noble and intellectual. It was not that mere physical admiration of beauty that is born of the senses, and that dies when the senses tire. It was such love as Michael Angelo had known, and Montaigne, and Winckelmann, and Shakespeare himself.

Basil translates these highly emotional and physical feelings into his art; his act of painting is an expression of his love for Dorian. This romantic devotion to Dorian becomes clear when he admits his reason for not wanting to exhibit the painting: he fears that people will see his "idolatry."

Dorian reflects, for a moment, that with this love Basil might have saved him from Lord Henry's influence, but he soon resigns himself to living a life dictated by the pursuit of passion. He devours the mysterious "yellow book" that Lord Henry gives him, which acts almost as a guide for the journey on which he is to travel. Like the protagonist of that novel, Dorian spirals into a world of self-gratification and exotic sensations. Although Wilde, in letters, identified the novel as imaginary, it is based in part on the nineteenth-century French novel *À Rebours* ("Against the Grain" or "Against Nature"), by Joris-Karl Huysmans, in which a decadent and wealthy Frenchman indulges himself in a host of bizarre sensory experiences. The yellow book has profound influence on Dorian; one might argue that it leads to his downfall. This downfall occurs not because the book itself is immoral (one need only recall the Preface's insistence that "[t]here is no such thing as a moral or an immoral book") but because Dorian allows the book to dominate and determine his actions so completely. It becomes, for Dorian, a doctrine as limiting and stultifying as the common Victorian morals from which he seeks escape. After all, Lord Henry is a great fan of the yellow book, but, to his mind, it is no greater or more important than any other work of notable art. He does not let it dominate his life or determine his actions, which, in turn, allows him to retain the respectability that Dorian soon loses.

CHAPTERS ELEVEN–TWELVE

SUMMARY: CHAPTER ELEVEN

Under the influence of the "yellow book," Dorian's character begins to change. He orders nearly a dozen copies of the first edition and has them bound in different colors to suit his shifting moods. Years pass. Dorian remains young and beautiful, but he is trailed by rumors that he indulges in dark, sordid behavior. Most people cannot help but dismiss these stories, since Dorian's face retains an unblemished look of "purity" and "innocence." Dorian delights in the ever-widening gulf between the beauty of his body and the corruption of his soul. He reflects that too much of human experience has been sacrificed to "asceticism" and pledges to live a life devoted to discovering "the true nature of the senses." Always intellectually curious, Dorian keeps up on the theories of the day—from mysticism to antinomianism to Darwinism—but he never lets these theories dominate him or interfere with his experiences. He devotes himself to the study of beautiful things: perfumes and their psychological effects, music, jewelry, embroideries, and tapestries.

Dorian continues to watch the painted image of himself age and deteriorate. Sometimes the sight of the portrait fills him with horror, while other times he reflects joyfully on the burdens that his body has been spared. But he fears that someone will break into his house and steal the painting; he knows many men who whisper of scandal behind his back and would delight in his downfall.

SUMMARY: CHAPTER TWELVE

On the eve of his thirty-eighth birthday, Dorian runs into Basil on a fog-covered street. He tries to pass him unrecognized, but Basil calls out to him and accompanies him home. Basil mentions that he is about to leave for a six-month stay in Paris but felt it necessary to stop by and warn Dorian that terrible rumors are being spread about his conduct. Basil reminds Dorian that there are no such things as "secret vices": sin, he claims, "writes itself across a man's face." Having said these words, he demands to know why so many of Dorian's friendships have ended disastrously. We learn that one boy committed suicide, and others had their careers or reputations ruined. Basil chastises Dorian for his influence over these unfortunate youths and urges him to use his considerable sway for good rather than evil. He adds that he wonders if he knows Dorian at all and wishes he were able to see the man's soul. Dorian laughs bitterly and says that the artist shall have his wish. He promises to show Basil his soul, which, he notes, most people believe only God can see. Basil decries Dorian's speech as blasphemous, and he begs Dorian to deny the terrible charges that have been made against him. Smiling, Dorian offers to show Basil the diary of his life, which he is certain will answer all of Basil's questions.

ANALYSIS: CHAPTERS ELEVEN–TWELVE

In the eighteen years that pass over the course of these two chapters, Dorian undergoes a profound psychological and behavioral transformation, though he remains the same physically. Although his behavior is, in part, a function of the Gothic nature of Wilde's tale—his mysterious, potentially dangerous behavior contributes to the novel's darkness—Dorian does not simply devolve into a villain. Though he exhibits inhuman behavior as he carelessly tosses aside his protégés (and his sins are only to become worse), he never completely sheds his conscience. This divide further manifests itself in that when Dorian looks at the painting of his dissipated self, he "sometimes loath[es] it and himself," while at other times he is overwhelmed by "that pride of individualism that is half the fascination of sin, and smil[es] with secret pleasure at the misshapen shadow that had to bear the burden that should have been his own." This tension points to the conflicted nature of Dorian's character.

We might consider Dorian's search for artistic and intellectual enlightenment—much of which is catalogued in Chapter Eleven—an attempt to find refuge from the struggle between mindless egotism and gnawing guilt. Indeed, Dorian lives a life marked by fear and suspicion. He finds it difficult to leave London, giving up the country villa he shares with Lord Henry for fear that someone will stumble upon the dreaded portrait in his absence. One can argue that Dorian turns to the study of perfumes, jewels, musical instruments, and tapestries as a source of comfort.

Certainly Dorian's greatest reason for indulging in the studies that Wilde describes at length is his disenchantment with the age in which he lives. Commonly referred to as the fin-de-siècle (French for "end of the century") period, the 1890s in England and Europe were marked by a world-weary sensibility that sought to free humanity from "the asceticism that deadens the senses." In art, this so-called asceticism referred primarily to artistic styles known as naturalism and realism, both of which aimed at reproducing the world as it is and ascribed a moral purpose to art. Dorian, taking the teachings of Lord Henry and the mysterious yellow book as scripture, believes that hedonism is the means by which he will rise above the "harsh, uncomely puritanism" of his age. This philosophy counters "any theory or system that would involve the sacrifice of any mode of passionate experience," which echoes the Preface's insistence that artists should not make distinctions between virtue and vice. According to this line of thinking, an experience is valuable in and of itself, regardless of its moral implications. Certainly, as Dorian lives his life under the rubric of aesthetic philosophy, he comes to appreciate the seductive beauty of the darker side of life, feeling "a curious delight in the thought that Art, like Nature, has her monsters, things of bestial shape and with hideous voices."

A possible seed of Dorian's undoing might be his intellectual development. Dorian is supposedly the personification of a type—a perfect blend of the scholar and the socialite—who lives his life, as Lord Henry dictates, as an individualist. Indeed, we are told that "no theory of life seemed to him to be of any importance compared with life itself." But. paradoxically. even the tenets of Dorian's "new Hedonism" prove constricting. It appears that he may have allowed himself to be too strongly influenced by Lord Henry and the yellow book, and that the philosophy of hedonism, meant to spare its followers from the conformities of dulling Victorian morality, may have simply become another, equally limiting doctrine.

CHAPTERS THIRTEEN–FOURTEEN

SUMMARY: CHAPTER THIRTEEN

Dorian leads Basil to the room in which he keeps the painting locked. Inside, Dorian lights a candle and tears the curtain back to reveal the portrait. The painting has become hideous, a "foul parody" of its former beauty. Basil stares at the horrifying painting in shock: he recognizes the brushwork and the signature as his own.

Dorian stands back and watches Basil with "a flicker of triumph in his eyes." When Basil asks how such a thing is possible, Dorian reminds him of the day he met Lord Henry, whose cautionary words about the ephemeral nature of beauty caused Dorian to pledge his soul for eternal, unblemished youth. Basil curses the painting as "an awful lesson," believing he worshipped the youth too much and is now being punished for it. He begs Dorian to kneel and pray for forgiveness, but Dorian claims it is too late. Glancing at his picture, Dorian feels hatred welling up within him. He seizes a knife and stabs Basil repeatedly. He then opens the door and listens for the sound of anyone stirring. When he is satisfied that no one has heard the murder, he locks the room and returns to the library. Dorian hides Basil's belongings in a secret compartment in the wall, then slips quietly out to the street. After a few moments, he returns, waking his servant and thus creating the impression that he has been out all night. The servant reports that Basil has been to visit, and Dorian says he is sorry to have missed him.

Summary: Chapter Fourteen

The next morning, Dorian wakes from a restful sleep. Once the events of the previous night sink in, he feels the return of his hatred for Basil. He decides not to brood on these things for fear of making himself ill or mad. After breakfast, he sends for Alan Campbell, a young scientist and former friend from whom he has grown distant. While waiting for Campbell to arrive, Dorian passes the time with a book of poems and reflects on his once intimate relationship with the scientist: the two were, at one point, inseparable. He also draws pictures and reflects on his drawings' similarity to Basil's likeness. Dorian then wonders if Campbell will come and is relieved when the servant announces his arrival.

Campbell has come reluctantly, having been summoned on a matter of life and death. Dorian confesses that there is a dead man locked in the uppermost room of his house, though he refrains from discussing the circumstances of the man's death. He asks Campbell to use his knowledge of chemistry to destroy the body. Campbell refuses. Dorian admits that he murdered the man, and Campbell reiterates that he has no interest in becoming involved. Dorian blackmails Campbell, threatening to reveal a secret that would bring great disgrace on him. With no alternative, Campbell agrees to dispose of the body and sends a servant to his home for the necessary equipment. Dorian goes upstairs to cover the portrait and notices that one of the hands on the painting is dripping with red, "as though the canvas had sweated blood." Campbell works until evening, then leaves. When Dorian returns to the room, the body is gone, and the odor of nitric acid fills the room.

ANALYSIS: CHAPTERS THIRTEEN–FOURTEEN

Chapters Thirteen and Fourteen take a decided turn for the macabre: the murder of Basil and the gruesome way it is reflected in the portrait—"as though the canvas had sweated blood"— root the novel firmly in the Gothic tradition, where darkness and supernatural horrors reign. In this setting, it becomes a challenge for Wilde to keep his hero from becoming a flat archetype of menacing evil. Much to his credit, he manages to keep Dorian a somewhat sympathetic character, even as he commits an unspeakable crime and blackmails a once dear friend to help him cover it up. Dorian remains worthy of sympathy because we see clearly the failure of his struggle to rise above a troubled conscience. With a murder added to his growing list of sins, Dorian wants nothing more than to be able to shrug off his guilt: he perceives Basil's corpse as a "thing" sitting in a chair and tries to lose himself in the lines of a French poet. The most telling evidence of Dorian's guilt can be seen as he sits waiting for the arrival of Alan Campbell; Dorian draws and soon remarks that "every face that he drew seemed to have a fantastic likeness to Basil Hallward." This scene resonates with the Chapter Nine scene in which Dorian asks the artist to draw a picture of Sibyl Vane so that he may better remember her: in both instances, the hedonistic Dorian betrays his gnawing conscience.

Throughout the novel, Basil acts as a sort of moral ballast, reminding Lord Henry and Dorian of the price that must be paid for their pleasure seeking. In these chapters, he provides a fascinating counterpoint to the philosophy by which Dorian lives. Refusing to believe that the dissipation of a soul can occur without notice, he claims that "[i]f a wretched man has a vice, it shows itself in the lines of his mouth, the droop of his eyelids, the moulding of his hands even." The introduction of such an opposing view discloses Wilde's love of contradiction. In his essay "The Truth of Masks," Wilde wrote that "[a] Truth in art is that whose contradictory is also true." Indeed, the truth of *The Picture of Dorian Gray*, if one is to be found, emerges from oppositions. After all, as Dorian reflects while gazing upon his ruined portrait, art depends as much upon horror as it does upon "marvellous beauty," just as one's being is always the synthesis of a "Heaven and Hell."

Like the other secondary characters in the novel, Alan Campbell is introduced and rather quickly ignored. His appearance, however, plays a vital role in establishing the darkening mood of the novel. The macabre experiments that he is accustomed to conducting as a chemist provide him with the knowledge that Dorian finds so necessary. Furthermore, the secrets that surround his personal life contribute to the air of mystery that surrounds Dorian. It is significant that the reader never learns the details of the circumstances by which Dorian blackmails Campbell. Given Wilde's increasingly indiscreet lifestyle and the increasingly hostile social attitudes toward homosexuality that flourished at the end of the nineteenth century, the reader can assume that Campbell's transgression is of a sexual nature. In 1885, the British Parliament passed the Labouchere Amendment, which widened prohibitions against male homosexual acts to include not only sodomy (which was punishable by death until 1861) but also "gross indecency" (meaning oral sex), an offense that carried a two-year prison term. Oscar Wilde himself was eventually found guilty of the latter offense. This new law was commonly known as the Blackmailer's Charter. Thus, Alan Campbell, a seemingly inconsequential character, serves as an important indicator of the social prejudices and punishments in Wilde's time.

CHAPTERS FIFTEEN–SIXTEEN

SUMMARY: CHAPTER FIFTEEN

That evening, Dorian goes to a dinner party, at which he flirts with bored noblewomen. Reflecting on his calm demeanor, he feels "keenly the terrible pleasure of a double life." Lady Narborough, the hostess, discusses the sad life of her daughter, who lives in a region of the countryside that has not witnessed a scandal since the time of Queen Elizabeth. Dorian finds the party tedious and brightens only when he learns Lord Henry will be in attendance.

During dinner, after Lord Henry has arrived, Dorian finds it impossible to eat. Lord Henry asks him what is the matter. Lady Narborough suggests that Dorian is in love, though Dorian assures her that she is wrong. The party-goers talk wittily about marriage, and the ladies then leave the gentlemen to their "politics and scandal." Lord Henry and Dorian discuss a party to be held at Dorian's country estate. Lord Henry then casually asks about Dorian's whereabouts the night before; Dorian's calm facade cracks a bit and he snaps out a strange, defensive response. Rather than join the women upstairs, Dorian decides to go home early.

Once Dorian arrives home, he retrieves Basil's belongings from the wall compartment and burns them. He goes to an ornate cabinet and, opening one of its drawers, draws out a canister of opium. At midnight, he dresses in common clothes and hires a coach to bring him to a London neighborhood where the city's opium dens prosper.

SUMMARY: CHAPTER SIXTEEN

As the coach heads toward the opium dens, Dorian recites to himself Lord Henry's credo: "To cure the soul by means of the senses, and the senses by means of the soul." He decides that if he cannot be forgiven for his sins, he can at least forget them; herein lies the appeal of the opium dens and the oblivion they promise. The coach stops, and Dorian exits. He enters a squalid den and finds a youth named Adrian Singleton, whom rumor says Dorian corrupted. As Dorian prepares to leave, a woman addresses him as "the devil's bargain" and "Prince Charming." At these words, a sailor leaps to his feet and follows Dorian to the street. As he walks along, Dorian wonders whether he should feel guilty for the impact he has had on Adrian Singleton's life. His meditation is cut short, however, when he is seized from behind and held at gunpoint. Facing him is James Vane, Sibyl's brother, who has been tracking Dorian for years in hopes of avenging Sibyl's death. James does not know Dorian's name, but the reference to "Prince Charming" makes him decide that it must be the man who wronged his sister. Dorian points out, however, that the man James seeks was in love with Sibyl eighteen years ago; since he, Dorian, has the face of a twenty-year-old man, he cannot possibly be the man who wronged Sibyl. James releases him and makes his way back to the opium den. The old woman tells James that Dorian has been coming there for eighteen years and that his face has never aged a day in all that time. Furious at having let his prey escape, James resolves to hunt him down again.

ANALYSIS: CHAPTERS FIFTEEEN–SIXTEEN

When Lord Henry alludes to the "*[f]in de siècle*" (or "end of the century") in Chapter Fifteen, he refers more to the sensibilities that flourished in the 1890s than the chronological time period. In this decade, many people in continental Europe and England felt an unshakable sense of discontent. The values that once seemed to structure life and give it meaning were apparently lost. Two main reasons for this disenchantment were linked to the public functions of art and morality, which, in Victorian England, seemed inextricably connected. Art, it was thought, should function as a moral barometer; to the minds of many, this dictum left room for only the most restrictive morals and the most unimaginative art. The term "fin de siècle" therefore came to describe a mode of thinking that sought to escape this disenchantment and restore beauty to art and reshape (and broaden) public understandings of morality.

In a way, though Dorian lives a life very much in tune with fin-de-siècle thinking, he rejects Victorian morals in favor of self-determined ethics based on pleasure and experience, and he retains—and is tortured by—a very Victorian mind-set. Indeed, by viewing the painting of himself as "the most magical of mirrors," Dorian disavows the tenets of aestheticism that demand that art be completely freed of its connection to morality. The picture becomes the gauge by which Dorian measures his downfall and serves as a constant reminder of the sins that plague his conscience. If we understand Dorian as a victim of this Victorian circumstance, we can read his drastic course of action in a more sympathetic light. Indeed, by Chapter Sixteen, he is a man desperate to forget the sins for which he believes he can never be forgiven. As he sinks into the sordidness of the London docks and their opium dens, he reflects:

> Ugliness was the one reality. The coarse brawl, the loathsome den, the crude violence of disordered life, the very vileness of thief and outcast, were more vivid, in their intense actuality of impression, than all the gracious shapes of Art, the dreamy shadows of Song.

Here, Dorian's thoughts echo French poets like Charles Baudelaire and Arthur Rimbaud, who believed that the description of intense experience was the key to true beauty, even (or perhaps especially) when the experience itself was something sordid, ugly, or grotesque. Indeed, in this trip to the opium den, Dorian intends to do nothing less than "cure the soul by means of the senses, and the senses by means of the soul."

Of course, what Dorian finds in the opium den has a far less curative effect than he hopes. The presence of Adrian Singleton, a young man whose downfall and subsequent drug addiction is at least partially Dorian's fault, pains Dorian's conscience and makes it impossible for him to "escape from himself." The reintroduction of James Vane makes this idea of escape quite literal. The avenging brother is, admittedly, a rather weak (albeit convenient) plot device that Wilde added to his 1891 revision of the novel. If Dorian fears and wishes to escape from himself, we can consider James the physical incarnation of that fear: James exists to precipitate the troubled Dorian's final breakdown.

CHAPTERS SEVENTEEN–EIGHTEEN

SUMMARY: CHAPTER SEVENTEEN

A week later, Dorian entertains guests at his estate at Selby. He talks with Lord Henry, the Duchess of Monmouth, and her husband; they discuss the nature and importance of beauty. The duchess criticizes Lord Henry for placing too great a value on beauty. The conversation turns to love; Lord Henry maintains that love, like life, depends upon repeating a great experience over and over again. Dorian agrees and excuses himself from his company. Lord Henry chastises the duchess for her flirtations. Soon, they hear a groan from the other end of the conservatory. They rush to find that Dorian has fallen in a swoon. At dinner, Dorian feels occasional chills of terror as he recalls that, before fainting, he saw the face of James Vane pressed against the conservatory window.

SUMMARY: CHAPTER EIGHTEEN

The following day, Dorian does not leave the house. The thought of falling prey to James Vane dominates him: every time he closes his eyes, the image of James's face in the window reappears. He begins to wonder, though, if this apparition is a figment of his imagination. The idea that his conscience could assert such fearful visions terrifies Dorian and makes him wonder if he will get any rest.

On the third day after the incident, Dorian ventures out. He strolls along the grounds of his estate and feels reinvigorated. He reflects to himself that the anguish that recently kept him in bed is completely against his nature. He has breakfast with the duchess and then joins a shooting party in the park. While strolling along with the hunters, Dorian is captivated by the graceful movement of a hare and begs his companions not to shoot it. Dorian's companion laughs at Dorian's silliness and shoots at the hare. The gunshot is followed by the cry of a man in agony. Several men thrash their way into the bushes to discover that a man has been shot. Having taken "the whole charge of shot in his chest," the man has died instantly. As the hunters head back toward the house, Dorian shares his worry with Lord Henry that this episode is a "bad omen." Lord Henry dismisses such notions, assuring Dorian that destiny is "too wise or too cruel" to send us omens.

Attempting to lighten the mood, Lord Henry teases Dorian about his relationship with the duchess. Dorian assures Henry that there is no scandal to be had and utters, quite pathetically, "I wish I could love." He bemoans the fact that he is so concentrated on himself, on his own personality, that he is thus unable to love another person. He entertains the idea of sailing away on a yacht, where he will be safe. When the gentlemen come upon the duchess, Dorian leaves Lord Henry to talk to her and retires to his room. There, the head keeper comes to speak to Dorian. Dorian inquires about the man who was shot, assuming him to have been a servant, and offers to make provisions for the man's family. The head keeper reports that the man's identity remains a mystery. As soon as he learns that the man is an anonymous sailor, Dorian demands to see him. He rides to a farm where the body is being kept and identifies it as that of James Vane. He rides home with tears in his eyes, feeling safe.

ANALYSIS: CHAPTERS SEVENTEEN–EIGHTEEN

Lord Henry's belief, uttered after the fatal hunting accident, that "[d]estiny does not send us heralds. She is too wise or too cruel for that," contrasts with Dorian's experience. In many ways, Basil's portrait of Dorian illustrates how destiny shapes Dorian's life, for while Dorian himself remains immune to the effects of time, his ever-deteriorating likeness in the portrait is indeed an undeniable herald of his ultimate downfall. The picture interrupts the pleasant reality of Dorian's life to remind him of his soul's dissipation. Although the aestheticists believed that art existed for its own sake, Dorian's experience demonstrates the limitations of that view. The painting becomes almost immediately a physical manifestation of conscience; it shows Dorian what is right and what is wrong in a very literal sense, and he frequently inspects the painting after committing an immoral or unethical act to see exactly how his conscience interprets that act. Ultimately, then, and in contrast to Lord Henry's philosophies, *The Picture of Dorian Gray* emphasizes the relationship between art and morality.

In addition to complicating the reader's understanding of art, which, as the novel draws to its close, becomes complex and somewhat paradoxical, Wilde demonstrates his characteristic flair for comedy and biting social satire. In Chapter Seventeen, Dorian's conversation with the Duchess of Monmouth and Lord Henry testifies to one of the skills that made Wilde the most celebrated playwright of his day. His brilliantly witty dialogue is responsible for his status as one of the most effective practitioners of the comedy of manners. A comedy of manners revolves around the complex and sophisticated behavior of the social elite, among whom one's character is determined more by appearance than by moral behavior. Certainly, by this definition, Lord Henry becomes something of a hero in the novel, as, even by his own admission, he cares much more for the beautiful than for the good.

Given the increasing seriousness of Dorian's plight and the ever-darkening state of his mind, the bulk of Chapter Seventeen serves as comic relief, as the dialogue between the duchess and Lord Henry is light and full of witticisms. Their exchange points to the relatively shallow nature of their society, in which love and morality amount to an appreciation of surfaces: as another lady of society reminds Dorian in Chapter Fifteen, "you are made to be good—you look so good." Here, morality is a function not of action or belief but of mere appearances.

Lord Henry's dismissive conception of England as a land founded on beer, the Bible, and repressive, unimaginative virtues serves as biting commentary of traditional, middle-class English morality. According to Lord Henry, a population whose tastes run to malt liquor and whose morality is determined by Christian dogma is doomed to produce little of artistic value. His sentiments align with the aesthetics' desire to free themselves (and art) from the bonds of conventional morality and sensibilities. Sympathetic as Wilde himself was to Lord Henry's opinions, he provides here a vital counterpoint to these opinions: the duchess's criticism that Lord Henry values beauty too highly begs us to ask the same question of Dorian and the aesthetic philosophy that dominates his life.

Chapters Nineteen–Twenty

Art has no influence upon action. . . . The books that the world calls immoral are books that show the world its own shame.   *(See* Quotations*, p. 51)*

Summary: Chapter Nineteen

Several weeks have passed, it seems, and Lord Henry visits Dorian in his London home. Dorian claims that he wants to reform himself and be virtuous. As evidence of his newfound resolve, Dorian describes a recent trip to the country during which he passed up an opportunity to seduce and defile an innkeeper's innocent daughter. Lord Henry dismisses Dorian's intentions to reform, and he turns the conversation to other subjects—Alan Campbell's recent suicide and the continued mystery of Basil Hallward's disappearance. Dorian asks if Lord Henry has ever considered that Basil might have been murdered. Lord Henry dismisses the idea, noting that Basil lacked enemies. Dorian then asks: "What would you say, Harry, if I told you that I had murdered Basil?" Lord Henry laughs and responds that murder is too vulgar for a man like Dorian.

The conversation drifts away from Basil. Lord Henry then asks Dorian, "'[W]hat does it profit a man if he gain the whole world and lose'—how does the quotation run?—'his own soul'?" Dorian starts nervously; Lord Henry explains that he heard a street preacher posing this question to a crowd. He mocks the man in his typical fashion, but Dorian cuts him short, insisting that the soul is very real. Lord Henry laughs at the suggestion, wondering aloud how Dorian has managed to remain so young after all these years. He wishes he knew Dorian's secret and praises Dorian's life as being "exquisite." He commends Dorian's mode of living and begs him not to spoil it by trying to be virtuous. Dorian somberly asks his friend not to loan anyone else the "yellow book," which has had such a corrupting effect upon his own character, but Lord Henry discounts his "moraliz[ing]" and remarks that "[a]rt has no influence upon action. . . . The books that the world calls immoral are books that show the world its own shame." Before leaving, Lord Henry invites Dorian to visit him the next day.

SUMMARY: CHAPTER TWENTY

That night, Dorian goes to the locked room to look at his portrait. He hopes his decision to amend his life will have changed the painting, and he considers that perhaps his decision *not* to ruin the innkeeper's daughter's reputation will be reflected in the painted face. But when Dorian looks at his portrait, he sees there is no change—except that "in the eyes there was a look of cunning, and in the mouth the curved wrinkle of the hypocrite." He realizes his pitiful attempt to be good was no more than hypocrisy, an attempt to minimize the seriousness of his crimes that falls far short of atonement. Furious, he seizes a knife—the same weapon with which he killed Basil—and drives it into the portrait in an attempt to destroy it.

From below, Dorian's servants hear a cry and a clatter. Breaking into the room, they see the portrait, unharmed, showing Dorian Gray as a beautiful young man. On the floor is the body of an old man, horribly wrinkled and disfigured, with a knife plunged into his heart. It is not until the servants examine the rings on the old man's hands that they identify him as Dorian Gray.

ANALYSIS: CHAPTERS NINETEEN–TWENTY

The contrast between Lord Henry and Dorian in Chapter Nineteen is instructive. When the novel begins, Lord Henry appears as a figure of worldly wisdom who seduces the naïve Dorian with fawning compliments and a celebration of selfishness and hedonism. Now that Dorian has actually *lived* the philosophy that Lord Henry so eloquently champions, however, he stands as proof of the limitations—indeed, even the misguided notions—of that philosophy. In the novel's final pages, Dorian is world-weary and borne down by the weight of his sins, while Lord Henry seems almost childishly naïve as he repeats his long-held but poorly informed beliefs. When Dorian all but confesses to Basil's murder, Lord Henry flippantly dismisses him, since his worldview holds that "[c]rime belongs exclusively to the lower orders." Only Lord Henry, who has never actually done any of the things he has inspired Dorian to do, could have the luxury of this thought. By keeping himself free from sin, even as he argues the virtues of sinning, Lord Henry lacks the terrible awareness of guilt and its debilitating effects. While the street preacher's rhetorical question about earthly gain at the cost of spiritual loss (from the New Testament, Mark 8:36) haunts Dorian, it holds no real meaning for Lord Henry.

At this stage, however, not even truthful self-awareness is enough to save Dorian. In his final moments, he attempts to repent the murder of Basil, the suicides of Sibyl Vane and Alan Campbell, and his countless other sins by refraining from seducing and ruining a naïve village girl. The discrepancy between the enormity of his crimes and this minor act of contrition is too great. Furthermore, he realizes that he does not want to confess his sins but rather have them simply go away. The portrait reflects this hypocrisy and drives him to his final, desperate act. He decides it is better to destroy the last evidence of his sin—the painting of his soul—than face up to his own depravity. The depravity he seeks to destroy is, in essence, himself; therefore, by killing it, he kills himself.

The end of the novel suggests a number of possible interpretations of Dorian's death. It may be his punishment for living the life of a hedonist, and for prizing beauty too highly, in which case the novel would be a criticism of the philosophy of aestheticism. But it is just as possible that Dorian is suffering for having violated the creeds of aestheticism. In other words, one can argue that Dorian's belief that his portrait reflects the state of his soul violates the principles of aestheticism, since, within that philosophy, art has no moral component. This reading is more in keeping with Wilde's personal philosophies and with the events of his life. In fact, elements of *The Picture of Dorian Gray* have an almost prophetic ring to them. Like Basil Hallward, Wilde would meet a tragic end brought about by his unrestrained worship of a beautiful young man. Additionally, like Alan Campbell, whom Dorian blackmails with vague threats of exposed secrets, Wilde would be punished for sexual indiscretions. Given the public nature of Wilde's trial and entire life—he was, in many ways, the first celebrity personality—it is impossible to ignore these parallels while reading *The Picture of Dorian Gray*. In *De Profundis*, Wilde's long letter to his lover, written from prison, he admits the limitations of the modes of thought and living that structured his life:

> I let myself be lured into long spells of senseless and sensual ease. I amused myself with being a *flaneur*, a dandy; a man of fashion. . . . Tired of being on the heights, I deliberately went to the depths in the search for new sensation. What the paradox was to me in the sphere of thought, perversity became to me in the sphere of passion. Desire, at the end, was malady, or a madness, or both. I grew careless of the lives of

others, I took pleasure where it pleased me, and passed on. I forgot that every little action of the common day makes or unmakes character, and that therefore what one has done in the secret chamber one has someday to cry aloud on the house-tops. I ceased to be lord over myself. I was no longer the captain of my soul, and did not know it. I allowed pleasure to dominate me. I ended in horrible disgrace.

The philosophy that *The Picture of Dorian Gray* proposes can be extremely seductive and liberating. But Wilde's words here reveal that society, conscience, or more likely both together ultimately make living that philosophy extremely difficult and even painful.

Important Quotations Explained

1. *We are punished for our refusals. Every impulse that we strive to strangle broods in the mind, and poisons us. The body sins once, and has done with its sin, for action is a mode of purification.... Resist it, and your soul grows sick with longing for the things it has forbidden to itself, with desire for what its monstrous laws have made monstrous and unlawful. It has been said that the great events of the world take place in the brain. It is in the brain, and the brain only, that the great sins of the world take place also.*

Lord Henry begins his seduction of Dorian's mind with these words in Chapter Two. Lord Henry advocates a return to the "Hellenic ideal," to the sensibilities of ancient Greece where the appreciation of beauty reigned. He strikes a contrast between those glory days and the present mode of living, which, he believes, is marked by a morality that demands self-denial. The outcome of denial, he goes on to say, is only a stronger desire for that which has been denied. This passage is a bold challenge to conventional and restrictive Victorian morality; it dismisses the notion of sin as a figment of the imagination. Interestingly, if sin is relegated to the mind, as Lord Henry would have it, then it should follow that the body is free from the effects of sin. According to this line of thinking, Dorian's tragedy, then, is that he is unable to purge his "monstrous and unlawful" acts from his conscience. One must remember, however, that Lord Henry has failed to put his philosophy to the test. Although he is a great advocate of sin, he is hardly a sinner, and his understanding of the soul—sickened or otherwise—never incorporates the knowledge that Dorian gradually acquires.

2.   *"To be good is to be in harmony with one's self,"* he replied,
      touching the thin stem of his glass with his pale, fine-pointed
      fingers. "Discord is to be forced to be in harmony with
      others. One's own life—that is the important thing. As for
      the lives of one's neighbours, if one wishes to be a prig or a
      Puritan, one can flaunt one's moral views about them, but
      they are not one's concern. Besides, Individualism has really
      the higher aim. Modern morality consists in accepting the
      standard of one's age. I consider that for any man of culture
      to accept the standard of his age is a form of the grossest
      immorality."

As Dorian prepares, in Chapter Six, to escort Lord Henry and Basil
to the theater to see Sibyl Vane perform, Lord Henry chastises
Dorian for dismissing, in the face of love, all of his "wrong, fascinating, poisonous, delightful theories." Here, Lord Henry expounds
on the virtues of individualism, which dictate that one develop
according to one's own standards. His outlook relies on Darwinism,
a fashionable theory at the time that asserted that an organism's
development would be altered or impaired if it were made to adjust
to the standards of another organism. Lord Henry fancies that he
and Dorian are creatures that require different standards than the
masses in order to develop fully. Thus, he readily rejects modern
morality, which governs the many, in favor of a self-determined
morality that applies only to himself. Although far from a prig or a
Puritan, Lord Henry does spend an inordinate amount of time wor-
rying over Dorian's development. Contrary to the principle of individualism he takes the time to relate, he not only does his best to
insinuate himself between Dorian and Sibyl, but he also takes up
Dorian's proper social development as his pet cause.

3.   *Yes: there was to be, as Lord Henry had prophesied, a new
     Hedonism that was to re-create life, and to save it from that
     harsh, uncomely puritanism that is having, in our own day,
     its curious revival. It was to have its service of the intellect,
     certainly; yet it was never to accept any theory or system that
     would involve the sacrifice of any mode of passionate
     experience. Its aim, indeed, was to be experience itself, and
     not the fruits of experience, sweet or bitter as they might be.
     Of the asceticism that deadens the senses, as of the vulgar
     profligacy that dulls them, it was to know nothing. But it
     was to teach man to concentrate himself upon the moments
     of a life that is itself but a moment.*

This passage from Chapter Eleven describes how Dorian, adjusting
to the strange privilege that his portrait affords him, devotes himself
to acquiring as many experiences as possible. Here, in order to discover "the true nature of the senses," Dorian studies rare musical
instruments, the arts of jewelry and embroidery, and the psychological effects of perfume. In addition to these pursuits, he begins to
devote his time to more sordid affairs, the nature of which is never
perfectly clear. We learn, from Basil's subsequent confrontation,
that Dorian is connected with the downfall of numerous youths, all
of whom have been brought to shame (and some even driven to suicide) by their associations with Dorian. Whether the outcome of
these experiences is "sweet or bitter" is not the point of the philosophy by which Dorian lives; on the contrary, the experience itself is
what matters. This "new Hedonism" is a form of resistance against
the conventional morality that Lord Henry spends so much of his
time criticizing.

QUOTATIONS

4. *Society, civilized society at least, is never very ready to
    believe anything to the detriment of those who are both rich
    and fascinating. It feels instinctively that manners are of
    more importance than morals, and, in its opinion, the
    highest respectability is of much less value than the
    possession of a good chef. And, after all, it is a very poor
    consolation to be told that the man who has given one a bad
    dinner, or poor wine, is irreproachable in his private life.
    Even the cardinal virtues cannot atone for half-cold entrées,
    as Lord Henry remarked once, in a discussion on the
    subject; and there is possibly a good deal to be said for his
    view. For the canons of good society are, or should be, the
    same as the canons of art. Form is absolutely essential to it.
    It should have the dignity of a ceremony, as well as its
    unreality, and should combine the insincere character of a
    romantic play with the wit and beauty that make such plays
    delightful to us. Is insincerity such a terrible thing? I think
    not. It is merely a method by which we can multiply
    our personalities.*

This passage, taken from Chapter Eleven, is important because it
contains the novel's only lapse into first-person narration. Here,
Wilde appears from behind the scenes to comment on civilized society. He asks the reader if the insincerity necessary to conduct oneself
in polite society is "such a terrible thing," and admits that, in his
opinion, it is not. He points, rather unapologetically, to the surface
nature of the society in which he lives and repeats a favorite epigram
that he also includes in his play *Lady Windermere's Fan*: "manners
are of more importance than morals." Indeed, *The Picture of
Dorian Gray* fully supports the observations that Wilde makes in
this paragraph. Despite the corrupt nature of Dorian's soul and
despite his utter lack of an acceptable moral code, he continues to be
welcomed into society merely because he looks good.

QUOTATIONS

5. *"[Y]ou poisoned me with a book once. I should not forgive that. Harry, promise me that you will never lend that book to anyone. It does harm."*

"My dear boy, you are really beginning to moralize. You will soon be going about like the converted, and the revivalist, warning people against all the sins of which you have grown tired. You are much too delightful to do that... . As for being poisoned by a book, there is no such thing as that. Art has no influence upon action. It annihilates the desire to act. It is superbly sterile. The books that the world calls immoral are books that show the world its own shame."

This exchange between Dorian and Lord Henry takes place in Chapter Nineteen, as Dorian, flayed by his conscience, pledges to live a reformed life. Reflecting on the course of his past twenty years, he confronts Lord Henry, whom he believes is responsible for leading him astray. Dorian criticizes the yellow book that, years before, had such a profound influence over him, claiming that this book did him great harm. This accusation is, of course, alien to Wilde's philosophy of aestheticism, which holds that art cannot be either moral or immoral. Lord Henry says as much, refusing to believe that a book could have such power. While there is something seductive in his observation that "the world calls immoral . . . books that show the world its own shame," Lord Henry's words here are less convincing than other statements to the same effect that he makes earlier in the novel. In the latter stages of the novel, we know of Dorian's downfall, and we know that he is anything but "delightful." At this point, Lord Henry's praising of Dorian makes Lord Henry seem hopelessly naïve, the victim of a philosophy whose consequences elude him.

KEY FACTS

FULL TITLE
  The Picture of Dorian Gray

AUTHOR
  Oscar Wilde

TYPE OF WORK
  Novel

GENRE
  Gothic; philosophical; comedy of manners

LANGUAGE
  English

TIME AND PLACE WRITTEN
  1890, London

DATE OF FIRST PUBLICATION
  The first edition of the novel was published in 1890 in *Lippincott's Monthly Magazine.* A second edition, complete with six additional chapters, was published the following year.

PUBLISHER
  The 1891 edition was published by Ward, Lock & Company.

NARRATOR
  The narrator is anonymous.

POINT OF VIEW
  The point of view is third person, omniscient. The narrator chronicles both the objective or external world and the subjective or internal thoughts and feelings of the characters. There is one short paragraph where a first-person point of view becomes apparent; in this section, Wilde becomes the narrator.

TONE
  Gothic (dark, supernatural); sardonic; comedic

TENSE
  Past

SETTING (TIME)
1890s

SETTING (PLACE)
London, England

PROTAGONIST
Dorian Gray

MAJOR CONFLICT
Dorian Gray, having promised his soul in order to live a life of perpetual youth, must try to reconcile himself to the bodily decay and dissipation that are recorded in his portrait.

RISING ACTION
Dorian notices the change in his portrait after ending his affair with Sibyl Vane; he commits himself wholly to the "yellow book" and indulges his fancy without regard for his reputation; the discrepancy between his outer purity and his inner depravity surges.

CLIMAX
Dorian kills Basil Hallward.

FALLING ACTION
Dorian descends into London's opium dens; he attempts to express remorse to Lord Henry; he stabs his portrait, thereby killing himself.

THEMES
The purpose of art; the supremacy of youth and beauty; the surface nature of society; the negative consequences of influence

MOTIFS
The color white; the picture of Dorian Gray; homoerotic male relationships

SYMBOLS
The opium den; James Vane; the yellow book

FORESHADOWING
Mrs. Vane's failed marriage, as well as Sibyl's portrayal of Juliet from Shakespeare's tragedy *Romeo and Juliet,* foreshadow the doomed nature of Sibyl's relationship with Dorian Gray.

KEY FACTS

STUDY QUESTIONS & ESSAY TOPICS

STUDY QUESTIONS

1. *Discuss the character of Lord Henry and his impact on Dorian.*

"Don't spoil him," Basil begs Lord Henry just before introducing him to Dorian. "Don't try to influence him. Your influence would be bad." But influence is what Lord Henry does best and what he enjoys most; inevitably, his charm, wit, and intellect hold tremendous sway over the impressionable Dorian. This influence, as Basil foresees, is primarily negative—if Dorian is like Faust, the fictional character who sells his soul for knowledge, then Lord Henry is something of a Mephistopheles, the devil who tempts Faust into the bargain. Lord Henry is a cynical aesthete, a lover of beauty with a contempt for conventional morality, and he views Dorian as a disciple with the potential to live out his philosophy of hedonism.

One must not overstate Lord Henry's role as a villain, however. Indeed, above all else, Lord Henry prizes individualism, which allows one to live one's life boldly, freely, and according to one's own edicts. Because Dorian so willingly assumes the role of disciple, the real source of his downfall rests in his willingness to sacrifice himself to another's vision. Following Lord Henry's advice and influenced by the "yellow book" that Lord Henry gives him, Dorian gradually allows himself to fall deep into a life of sin, all in the name of pursuing pleasure—which, according to Lord Henry, is the highest good. But, significantly, Lord Henry himself never seems to stray from the straight and narrow: he shocks cocktail guests with his ideas but never puts them into practice himself. He is a thinker, not a doer, and by the end of the novel, he seems curiously naïve about where his philosophy, if put into action, would lead him. Unwilling (or unable) to see the effects of his philosophy, he continues to champion his ideas even after they have ruined his protégé's life.

2.   *Discuss the role of homoeroticism in the novel.*

While Wilde's own homosexual inclinations were well known in his day, there is no explicit mention of homosexuality in the novel. In conservative 1890s England, such openness in print would have made the novel unpublishable. Some critics attacked the novel— even in its present form—as unmanly. Still, the homoerotic relationships between the male characters are vital to the novel. Initially, Basil's affection for Dorian, which has about it the obsessive and adoring qualities of romantic love, produces the painting that forms the heart of the novel. Certainly, Lord Henry's relationship to Dorian is also marked by a profound affection and is likened to a seduction: "He would seek to dominate him—had already, indeed, half done so." Meanwhile, when Dorian gives in to a life of sin, there is a strong suggestion that his numerous friendships with young men contain a homosexual element. Nowhere is this element more boldly suggested than through the character of Alan Campbell, whom Dorian blackmails into helping dispose of Basil's body. Given the era's tightening legal strictures against homosexual acts between men and the passage of a sodomy law that came to be known as the Blackmailer's Charter, the implication here is that the indiscretion Dorian threatens to expose is of a homosexual nature. Despite the dangers often involved in these affairs, Wilde viewed homoerotic relationships between men as a paragon of social virtue. Returning to the teachings of ancient Greece, where men and boys shared in sexual relationships, Wilde asserted that there was nothing nobler than this love, which he considered a pillar of Western culture and art.

3.   *"There is no such thing as a moral or an immoral book,"*
      Wilde says in the Preface. "Books are well written, or
      badly written. That is all." Does the novel confirm
      this argument?

The idea that there is no morality in art, only beauty (or an absence
of beauty, in the case of bad art), is the central tenet of a movement
known as aestheticism, which sought to free literature and other
forms of artistic expression from the burden of being ethical or
instructive. Wilde himself was associated closely with this creed, as
the Preface to *The Picture of Dorian Gray* makes clear. But the novel
that follows grapples with the philosophy of art for art's sake in a
complicated way. After all, the protagonist suffers from the lessons
he has learned from the yellow book that has "poisoned" him. Lord
Henry insists that a book can do no such thing, and we are left to
decide how much blame one can place on a book and how much
blame must be placed on the reader. Indeed, in one respect, *The Picture of Dorian Gray* seems to be a novel of extremely moral sensibilities, since Dorian suffers *because* he allows himself to be poisoned
by a book. In other words, he defies the artistic principles that structure the yellow book. One must wonder, then, if there is such a thing
as a book without some sort of moral or instruction.

SUGGESTED ESSAY TOPICS

1. *Discuss the relationship between Basil and Dorian.*

2. *Analyze the Gothic elements in* THE PICTURE OF DORIAN GRAY.

3. *Discuss the role of Sibyl Vane in the novel.*

4. *Discuss the parallels between Dorian's story and the Faust legend. Does Dorian make a pact with the devil?*

5. *Why does Dorian decide to destroy the painting at the end of the novel?*

6. *Compare and contrast the characters of Basil and Lord Henry. What is their relationship to one another? To Dorian?*

Review & Resources

Quiz

1. What famous phrase appears in the Preface to *The Picture of Dorian Gray*?

    A. "All happy families resemble one another, but each unhappy family is unhappy in its own way"
    B. "All art is quite useless"
    C. "The best way to get rid of a temptation is to yield to it"
    D. "It was the best of times, it was the worst of times"

2. What is Basil Hallward's occupation?

    A. Writer
    B. Chef
    C. Painter
    D. Sculptor

3. Why does Basil not wish to exhibit his portrait of Dorian?

    A. He thinks it is a poor work of art
    B. He feels he has put too much of himself into it
    C. Dorian Gray has asked him not to
    D. He plans to put it over his own mantelpiece

4. How does Basil first meet Dorian?

    A. Through a newspaper advertisement
    B. In an opium den
    C. When Lord Henry introduced them
    D. At a party hosted by Lady Brandon

5. What is the name of Sibyl's brother?

    A. James
    B. Christopher
    C. Wilfred
    D. Alan

6. When Dorian arrives at his studio, what request does Basil make of Lord Henry?

    A.   He asks Lord Henry not to mention the painting to Dorian

    B.   He begs Lord Henry not to influence Dorian

    C.   He asks Lord Henry not to tell Dorian his real name

    D.   He suggests that Lord Henry leave without meeting Dorian

7. What best describes the philosophy that Lord Henry espouses?

    A.   Hedonistic

    B.   Devoutly religious

    C.   Altruistic

    D.   Existential

8. Upon seeing his completed portrait, what does Dorian wish?

    A.   That he could take the painting home with him

    B.   That the painting would grow old while he remained eternally young

    C.   That the painting would bear the marks of his sins

    D.   That he looked as beautiful as the man in the painting

9. To whom does Basil give the painting?

    A.   Dorian

    B.   Lord Henry

    C.   Lady Agatha

    D.   The British Museum

10. What is Sibyl Vane's occupation?

    A.   Prostitute

    B.   Noblewoman

    C.   Poet

    D.   Actress

REVIEW & RESOURCES

11.   What is Sibyl's nickname for Dorian?

      A.   Lord Gray
      B.   Prince Charming
      C.   The Radiant Youth
      D.   Young Apollo

12.   On the night that Lord Henry and Basil come to see her act, what does Sibyl resolve to do?

      A.   Forget her lines
      B.   Convince them that she truly loves Dorian
      C.   Impress them with her best rendition of Juliet
      D.   Give up acting

13.   How does Dorian escape James Vane when James accosts him?

      A.   He draws a knife and threatens him
      B.   He points out that he is much too young to have been in love with Sibyl eighteen years before
      C.   He tells him that another man was responsible for Sibyl's suicide and gives him Basil's address
      D.   He apologizes to him for his actions, claiming that he has realized the errors of his youth

14.   After Sibyl's death, who convinces Dorian to have no involvement in the case?

      A.   Basil
      B.   Lord Henry
      C.   Mrs. Vane
      D.   Alan Campbell

15.   What gift from Lord Henry profoundly influences Dorian?

      A.   A statue
      B.   A piece of jewelry
      C.   A book
      D.   A painting

16. As the years pass, what happens to Dorian's body?

    A. It becomes horribly ugly
    B. It slowly disintegrates
    C. It remains youthful and beautiful
    D. It grows perpetually younger and stronger

17. Over which issue does Basil confront Dorian the night of Basil's death?

    A. Sibyl Vane's death
    B. The whereabouts of the portrait
    C. The rumors of Dorian's wicked behavior that are being spread in polite society
    D. Lord Henry's divorce

18. How does Dorian respond to Basil's confrontation?

    A. He shows Basil the horribly changed portrait
    B. He orders Basil to leave the house
    C. He laughs it all off
    D. He sends for the police

19. How does Dorian kill Basil?

    A. He stabs him to death
    B. He shoots him
    C. He pushes him out a window
    D. He chokes him

20. To whom does Dorian turn for help with disposing of Basil's body?

    A. Lord Henry
    B. Alan Campbell
    C. James Vane
    D. His servant

21. What is finally done with Basil's corpse?

    A. It is locked away in the attic of Dorian's home
    B. It is buried in Dorian's garden
    C. It is thrown into the Thames
    D. It is dissolved in acid

22. Where does Dorian first encounter James Vane?

    A.   In a brothel
    B.   At Dorian's country estate
    C.   In an opium den
    D.   In an art gallery

23. What does Dorian resolve to do when he notices a change in his portrait after breaking up with Sibyl?

    A.   Make amends with her
    B.   Live sinfully without regret
    C.   Bequeath his estate to the Vane family
    D.   Rip up the portrait

24. What fate befalls James Vane?

    A.   He is drowned in the Thames
    B.   He is accidentally killed by hunters at Dorian's country home
    C.   He is killed in a duel with Lord Henry
    D.   His ship is lost at sea

25. What happens when Dorian attempts to drive a knife into his portrait?

    A.   The weapon sinks into the canvas but cannot be pulled out again
    B.   The portrait is torn to bits, and the pieces show a beautiful young man once more
    C.   He is unable to bring himself to destroy the painting, and he throws the knife out the window
    D.   He becomes the disfigured image in the painting and, in effect, stabs himself

REVIEW & RESOURCES

ANSWER KEY:

1: B; 2: C; 3: B; 4: D; 5: A; 6: B; 7: A; 8: B; 9: A; 10: D; 11: B; 12: D; 13: B; 14: B; 15: C; 16: C; 17: C; 18: A; 19: A; 20: B; 21: D; 22: C; 23: A; 24: B; 25: D

Suggestions for Further Reading

ELLMANN, RICHARD, ed. *Oscar Wilde: A Collection of Critical Essays*. Englewood Cliffs, New Jersey: Prentice-Hall, 1969.

FIDO, MARTIN. *Oscar Wilde*. New York: Viking Press, 1973.

GILLESPIE, MICHAEL PATRICK. THE PICTURE OF DORIAN GRAY: *What the World Thinks Me*. New York: Twayne Publishers, 1995.

LIEBMAN, SHELDON W. "Character Design in *The Picture of Dorian Gray*." *Studies in the Novel* 31, no. 3. (1999): 296-316.

MCCORMACK, JERUSHA HULL. *The Man Who Was Dorian Gray*. New York: St. Martin's Press, 2000.

NICHOLLS, MARK. *The Importance of Being Oscar: The Life and Wit of Oscar Wilde*. New York: St. Martin's Press, 1980.

RABY, PETER, ed. *The Cambridge Companion to Oscar Wilde*. Cambridge: Cambridge University Press, 1997.

RIQUELME, JOHN PAUL. "Oscar Wilde's Aesthetic Gothic: Walter Pater, Dark Enlightenment, and *The Picture of Dorian Gray*." *Modern Fiction Studies* 46, no. 3 (2000): 609–631.

SAN JUAN, EPIFANIO. *The Art of Oscar Wilde*. Princeton, New Jersey: Princeton University Press, 1967.

WOMACK, KENNETH. "'Withered, Wrinkled, and Loathsome of Visage': Reading the Ethics of the Soul and the Late-Victorian Gothic in *The Picture of Dorian Gray*." In *Victorian Gothic: Literary and Cultural Manifestations in the Nineteenth Century*, edited by Ruth Robbins and Julian Wolfreys, 168–181. New York: Palgrave, 2000.

REVIEW & RESOURCES

SPARKNOTES
TEST PREPARATION
GUIDES

The SparkNotes team figured it was time to cut standardized tests down to size. We've studied the tests for you, so that SparkNotes test prep guides are:

Smarter
Packed with critical-thinking skills and test-
taking strategies that will improve your score.

Better
Fully up to date, covering all new features of the tests,
with study tips on every type of question.

Faster
Our books cover exactly what you need to
know for the test. No more, no less.

SparkNotes Guide to the SAT & PSAT
SparkNotes Guide to the SAT & PSAT—Deluxe Internet Edition
SparkNotes Guide to the ACT
SparkNotes Guide to the ACT—Deluxe Internet Edition
SparkNotes SAT Verbal Workbook
SparkNotes SAT Math Workbook
SparkNotes Guide to the SAT II Writing
5 More Practice Tests for the SAT II Writing
SparkNotes Guide to the SAT II U.S. History
5 More Practice Tests for the SAT II History
SparkNotes Guide to the SAT II Math Ic
5 More Practice Tests for the SAT II Math Ic
SparkNotes Guide to the SAT II Math IIc
5 More Practice Tests for the SAT II Math IIc
SparkNotes Guide to the SAT II Biology
5 More Practice Tests for the SAT II Biology
SparkNotes Guide to the SAT II Physics

SPARKNOTES™ LITERATURE GUIDES